LEARNING FROM
JESUS

OTHER RENOVARÉ RESOURCES

Connecting with God
by Lynda L. Graybeal and Julia L. Roller

Devotional Classics
co-edited by Richard J. Foster and James Bryan Smith

Embracing the Love of God
by James Bryan Smith

The Renovaré Spiritual Formation Bible
edited by Richard J. Foster and others

Songs for Renewal
by Janet Lindeblad Janzen with Richard J. Foster

Spiritual Classics
co-edited by Richard J. Foster and Emilie Griffin

A Spiritual Formation Journal
created by Jana Rea with Richard J. Foster

A Spiritual Formation Workbook
by James Bryan Smith with Lynda L. Graybeal

Streams of Living Water
by Richard J. Foster

Wilderness Time
by Emilie Griffin

OTHER BOOKS
BY RICHARD J. FOSTER

Celebrating the Disciplines
with Kathryn A. Helmers

Celebration of Discipline

The Challenge of the Disciplined Life

Freedom of Simplicity

Prayer: Finding the Heart's True Home

Prayers from the Heart

Richard J. Foster's Study Guide for Celebration of Discipline

Seeking the Kingdom

LEARNING FROM
JESUS

A SPIRITUAL FORMATION GUIDE

A RENOVARÉ RESOURCE

FOR INDIVIDUALS AND GROUPS

Introduction by Richard J. Foster

Lynda L. Graybeal and Julia L. Roller

HarperSanFrancisco
A Division of HarperCollinsPublishers

For information about RENOVARÉ write to RENOVARÉ, 8 Inverness Dr East, Suite 102, Englewood, CO 80112-5624 or log on to the Web site http://www.renovare.org.

HarperCollins books may be purchased for educational, business, or sales promotional use. For information please write: Special Markets Department, HarperCollins Publishers, 10 East 53rd Street, New York, NY 10022.

HarperCollins Web site: http://www.harpercollins.com

HarperCollins®, 📖®, and HarperSanFrancisco™
are trademarks of HarperCollins Publishers

FIRST EDITION
Designed by Sharon VanLoozenoord

Library of Congress Cataloging-in-Publication.

Graybeal, Lynda L.
 Learning from Jesus : a spiritual formation guide : a Renovaré resource / written by Lynda L. Graybeal and Julia L. Roller ; introduction by Richard J. Foster.— 1st ed.
 p. cm.
 ISBN-13: 978–0–06–084124–9
 ISBN-10: 0–06–084124–9
 1. Bible. N.T. Gospels—Criticism, interpretation, etc. 2. Bible. N.T. Gospels—Study and teaching. 3. Jesus Christ—Example—Study and teaching. I. Roller, Julia L. II. Title
 BS2555.52.G73   2006
 226'.0071—dc22   2006041205

06 07 08 09 10 RRD(H) 10 9 8 7 6 5 4 3 2 1

CONTENTS

INTRODUCTION

For five years I engaged in what is bound to be my life's richest adventure of biblical work. Five of us (in time to be called general editors) were wrestling with the whole of Scripture through the lens of spiritual formation, seeing what we could learn and how we could be formed and conformed and transformed ever more deeply in the subterranean chambers of the soul. That project eventually came into published form as *The Renovaré Spiritual Formation Bible*.

How do I describe to you the excitement of those early days? To be sure, it was genuine work, for the intensity of labor was exhausting, but it was so much more than "work." It was the thrill of creative ideas flying fast and furious, of dynamic insights crammed one upon another. In those chaotic sessions I often felt like I was astride a wild stallion at full gallop, gripping the mane for dear life.

But it wasn't just the excitement of new concepts emerging out of the wealth of pooled intellectual capital. No, it was the sense of awe before the majesty of Scripture, of being drawn in toward the Divine Center, of holy stillness, of quiet worship and whispered promptings. And prayers—morning prayers and evening prayers and days soaked in prayerful sharing over the sacred text. Oh yes, and laughter. Deep, side-splitting belly laughter. Holy hilarity I guess you could call it.

The experience was joyfully creative and soul-expanding. We knew we were onto something big—big ideas with huge consequences for the hearts and minds of precious people.

At some point in this dynamic process we began to ask if a way could be found to help those who would read this *Renovaré Bible* to experience something of the excitement and adventure we had in first hammering out the concepts of the "Immanuel Principle" and the "with-God life." Could others discover for themselves how the "with-God" framework illuminates God's purposes in history? How over many centuries and through multiple human authors, God has so superintended the development of the Bible that it speaks to us about real life (*zoë*) and teaches us how to live "with God" through the vicissitudes of human experience? How the aim of God in history is the creation of an all-inclusive community of loving persons, with God himself included in this community as its prime sustainer and most glorious inhabitant? How the unity of the Bible is discovered in the lived community reality of this *zoë* life under God and with God and through the power of God?

And so these spiritual formation guides were born. Together they will take us on a journey through the entire panorama of Scripture. Through these spiritual formation guides, we will discover how the Old Testament depicts God's pursuit of loving relationship with his chosen people, Israel, and how through Israel all the peoples of the earth are to be blessed. We see this "pursuit of loving relationship" carried on through the lives of the patriarchs, the history of the Israelites in their exodus from slavery and their entrance into the Promised Land, in the forming and then the disintegration of tribe and nation. Then, the New Testament depicts the story of God's fulfillment of "loving relationship" with a people who become God's own through their identity in Jesus Christ: "God's household, having been built upon the foundation of the apostles and prophets, Christ Jesus Himself being the corner *stone,* in whom the whole building, being fitted together, is growing into a holy temple in the Lord; in whom you also are being built together into a dwelling of God in the Spirit" (Eph 2:19–22, NASB).

As the Bible closes, it opens a window onto the fulfillment of God's purposes for humanity beyond human history: "Now the dwelling of God is with human beings, and he will live with them. They will be his people, and God himself will be with them and be their God" (Rev 21:3, NIVI).

Thus, we will discover that the Immanuel Principle is, after all, a cosmic principle that God has used all along in creation and redemption. It alone serves to guide human life aright on earth now and even illuminates the future of the universe. Of course, the few examples I have shared here hardly touch the surface of the great river of life that flows from God through Scripture and into the thirsty wastelands of the human soul. "Let anyone who is thirsty come to me [Jesus] and drink. Whoever believes in me, as the Scripture has said, will have streams of living water flowing from within" (John 7:37–38, NIVI).

This study guide, therefore, has been created to help each of us enter into the story of the Bible so as to see our own story, our own journey in the great cosmic drama of divine-human relationship. May you, may I, choose to surrender freely to this river of life, receiving and helping others to receive this Life, this *Zoë,* as our own.

Richard J. Foster

HOW TO USE THIS GUIDE

This book is dedicated to nurturing spiritual formation through the study of Scripture. Devotional excerpts from the writings of ancient and contemporary Christians; questions for reflection; and exercises centered around Spiritual Disciplines, such as study, prayer, solitude, meditation, and silence; supplement and illumine the biblical text. This book is not intended to be read passively; it requires the interactive participation of you the reader. To engage with the texts we have chosen and to do the exercises we have set out here will require time and dedication beyond mere reading of the guide. We hope you will accept this challenge!

Whether you are using the guide as an individual or as a group, we recommend that you begin by reading "The With-God Life" and becoming familiar with the accompanying chart, which will give you some insight into the role of Scripture in the process of spiritual formation. Then you should read the Overview, which will give you a sense of the main themes we discuss. The material in the chapters of this guide is intended to help you take the next step—to engage in activities that will help you grow closer to God.

INSTRUCTIONS FOR INDIVIDUALS

Because this book is an interactive guide for spiritual formation, we recommend that you read it more slowly than you would another kind of book. Read the Devotional and Scripture Readings and the My Life with God Exercise at the beginning of each chapter, then try to give yourself at least a week to do the exercise before reading the rest of the chapter. You may want to use a journal or notebook to record your responses to the questions in the chapter. Move on to a new chapter when you feel ready.

INSTRUCTIONS FOR GROUPS

If this is your first time participating in a spiritual formation group, your first question is likely: What is a spiritual formation group, anyway? Simply put, a spiritual formation group consists of two to seven people who meet together on a regular basis, bringing challenge and focus to their spiritual lives. Through mutual encouragement and accountability, spiritual formation groups enable their members to assist one another on the road of discipleship to Jesus Christ. We need encouragement during the times when we succeed and the times when we fail in our life of discipleship. We need others to keep us accountable, to remind us to continually pursue our lives with God and our discipleship to Jesus. Each is a natural by-product of the spiritual formation group experience.

If you are just starting a group, try recruiting one or two friends and asking each to recruit one other person. You could also place an ad in your church bulletin or make an announcement at your weekly service. Try to limit your group to seven people or fewer. With a larger group, meetings tend to run too long and not all members participate equally. Four or five people is optimal.

Plan for at least twelve group meetings, each dedicated to a chapter. (You might choose to have an additional introductory meeting or an extra final meeting for evaluation and making future plans.) Meet as often as once a week or as infrequently as once a month, whatever is best for your group. Each meeting should last sixty to ninety minutes. Although you may want to designate someone to be in charge of initial logistics and communication about meeting times and places, we have designed these guides to work in a leaderless format. Each week a different person serves as a facilitator to keep the discussion moving along. No extra study or preparation is required for that person; he or she simply follows the group directions in the margins of each chapter.

Before the first meeting, each member should read the Devotional and Scripture Readings and do the My Life with God Exercise in the first chapter. Because of these requirements and to make group meetings easier, it is helpful for each member of the group to have their own copy of this book. Members read ahead in this way before every meeting. The exercises are quite involved and require a time commitment of at least a few minutes each day over several days. Allow at least a week for members to do the exercise before holding the first meeting. Some may wish to read through the entire chapter beforehand, but it is not necessary to do so.

At the end of each chapter are additional exercises, resources, and reflection questions. These optional sections are primarily intended for individual use after the group meeting. Some may enjoy writing out answers to the reflection questions in the extra space provided or in their journals or notebooks. But if your group is quite interested in a particular chapter, you might consider incorporating the Additional Reflection Questions into your group meeting.

Now you are ready to form your group and plan your first meeting! May God bless you richly in this endeavor.

Lynda L. Graybeal and Julia L. Roller

THE WITH-GOD LIFE

Adapted from an essay in The Renovaré Spiritual Formation Bible *by Gayle Beebe, Richard J. Foster, Lynda L. Graybeal, Thomas C. Oden, and Dallas Willard*

CATCHING THE VISION: THE LIFE

The Bible is all about human life "with God." It is about how God has made this "with-God" life possible and will bring it to pass. In fact, the name Immanuel, meaning in Hebrew "God is with us," is the title given to the one and only Redeemer because it refers to God's everlasting intent for human life—namely, that we should be in every aspect a dwelling place of God. *Indeed, the unity of the Bible is discovered in the development of life with God as a reality on earth, centered in the person of Jesus.* We might call this the *Immanuel Principle* of life.

This dynamic, pulsating, with-God life is on nearly every page of the Bible. To the point of redundancy, we hear that *God is with* his people: with Abraham and Moses, with Esther and David, with Isaiah, Jeremiah, Amos, Micah, Haggai, and Malachi, with Mary, Peter, James, and John, with Paul and Barnabas, with Priscilla and Aquila, with Lydia, Timothy, Epaphroditus, Phoebe, and with a host of others too numerous to name.

Accordingly, the primary purpose of the RENOVARÉ guides is to enable us to see and understand the reality of the "with-God" life, to enter the process of the transformation of our whole person and of our whole life into *Christlikeness*.

Opening Ourselves to the Life

If we want to receive from the Bible the life "with God" that is portrayed *in* the Bible, we must be prepared to have our dearest and most fundamental assumptions about ourselves and our associations called into question. We must read humbly and in a constant attitude of repentance. Only in this way can we gain a thorough and practical grasp of the spiritual riches that God has made available to all humanity in his written Word.

When we turn to Scripture in this way, our reason for "knowing" the Bible and everything it teaches is that we might love more and know more of love.

We experience this love not as an abstraction but as a practical reality that possesses us. And because all those who love thoroughly obey the law, we would become ever more obedient to Jesus Christ and his Father.

Our goal is not to control the Bible—that is, to try to make it "come out right"—but simply to release its life into our lives and into our world. We seek to trust the living water that flows from Christ through the Bible, to open ourselves to this living water and to release it into the world as best we can, and then get out of its way.

NURTURING THE INTENTION: THE BIBLE

God remains with the Bible always. It is God's book. No one owns it but God himself. It is the loving heart of God made visible and plain. And receiving this message of exquisite love is the great privilege of all who long for life with God. *Reading, studying, memorizing, and meditating upon Scripture has always been the foundation of the Christian disciplines.* All of the disciplines are built upon Scripture. Our practice of the Spiritual Disciplines is kept on course by our immersion in Scripture. And so it is, we come to see, that this reading, studying, memorizing, and meditating is totally in the service of "the life which is life indeed" (1 Tim 6:19, RSV). We long with all our heart to know *for ourselves* this with-God kind of life that Jesus brings in all its fullness.

And the Bible has been given to help us. God has so superintended the writing of Scripture that it serves as a most reliable guide for our spiritual formation. But God uses human action in its presentation to the world, just as it is authored by humans. Thus we must consider how we ourselves can come to the Bible and also how we can present it to all peoples in a way that inducts the soul into the eternal kind of life.

We begin by finding experientially, day by day, how to let Jesus Christ live in every dimension of our being. In Christian community, we can open our lives to God's life by gathering regularly in little groups of two or more to encourage one another to discover the footprints of God in our daily existence and to venture out *with God* into areas where we have previously walked alone or not at all.

But the aim is not external conformity, whether to doctrine or deed, but the re-formation of the inner self—of the spiritual core, the place of thought and feeling, of will and character. The psalmist cries, "You desire truth in the inward being; therefore teach me wisdom in my secret heart.... Create in me a clean heart, O God, and put a new and right spirit within me" (Ps 51:6, 10). It is the "inner person" that is being "*renewed [renovaré]* day by day" (2 Cor 4:16, emphasis added).

While the many Christian traditions differ over the details of spiritual formation, they all come out at the same place: the transformation of the person into Christlikeness. "Spiritual formation" is the process of transforming the inner reality of the self (the *inward being* of the psalmist) in such a way that the overall life with God seen in the Bible naturally and freely comes to pass in us. Our inner world (the *secret heart*) becomes the home of Jesus, by his initiative and our response. As a result, our interior world becomes increasingly like the inner self of Jesus and, therefore, the natural source of words and deeds that are characteristic of him. By his enabling presence, we come to "let the same mind be in you that was in Christ Jesus" (Phil 2:5).

UNDERSTANDING THE MEANS:
THE SPIRITUAL DISCIPLINES

This "with-God" life we find in the Bible is the very life to which we are called. In fact, it is exactly the life Jesus is referring to when he declares, "I am come that they might have life, and that they might have *it* more abundantly" (John 10:10, KJV). It is a life of unhurried peace and power. It is solid. It is serene. It is simple. It is radiant. It takes no time, though it permeates all of our time.

But such a life does not simply fall into our hands. Frankly, it is no more automatic for us than it was for those luminaries who walk across the pages of the Bible. There is a God-ordained way to become the kind of people and communities that can fully and joyfully enter into such abundant living. And this involves intentionally "train[ing] ... in godliness" (1 Tim 4:7). This is the purpose of the *disciplines* of the spiritual life. Indeed, the very reason for these spiritual formation guides is so that Scripture may be the primary means for the discovery, instruction, and practice of the Spiritual Disciplines, which bring us all the more fully into the with-God life.

The Spiritual Disciplines, then, are the God-ordained means by which each of us is enabled to bring the little, individualized power-pack we all possess—we call it the human body—and place it before God as "a living sacrifice" (Rom 12:1). It is the way we go about training in the spiritual life. By means of this process we become, through time and experience, the kind of person who naturally and freely expresses "love, joy, peace, patience, kindness, generosity, faithfulness, gentleness, and self-control" (Gal 5:22–23).

Many and Varied

What are these Spiritual Disciplines? They include fasting and prayer, study and service, submission and solitude, confession and worship, meditation and silence, simplicity, frugality, secrecy, sacrifice, and celebration. Such Spiritual Disciplines crop up repeatedly in the Bible as the way God's people trained themselves and were trained by God to achieve godliness. And not only in the Bible: the saints down through history, and even spilling over into our own time, have all practiced these ways of "grow[ing] in grace" (2 Pet 3:18).

A Spiritual Discipline is an intentionally directed action by which we do what we *can* do in order to receive from God the ability (or power) to do what we cannot achieve by direct effort. It is not in us, for example, to love our enemies. We might try very hard to love our enemies, but we will fail miserably. Always. This strength, this power to love our enemies—that is, to genuinely and uncon-ditionally love those who curse us and spitefully use us—is simply not within our natural abilities. We cannot do it by ourselves. Ever.

But this *fact of life* does not mean that we do nothing. Far from it! Instead, by an act of the will we choose to take up disciplines of the spiritual life that we can do. These disciplines are all actions of body, mind, and spirit that are within our power. Not always and not perfectly, to be sure. But they are things we can do. By choice. By choosing actions of *fasting, study, solitude,* and so forth.

Their Purpose

The Spiritual Disciplines in and of themselves have no merit whatsoever. They possess no righteousness, contain no rectitude. Their purpose—their only purpose—is to place us before God. After that they have come to the end of their usefulness. But it is enough. Then the grace of God steps in and takes this simple offering of ourselves and creates out of it a person who embodies the goodness of God—indeed, a person who can come to the place of truly loving even enemies.

Again, Spiritual Disciplines involve doing what we *can* do to receive from God the power to do what we cannot do. And God graciously uses this process to produce in us the kind of person who automatically will do what needs to be done when it needs to be done.

Now, this ability to do what needs to be done when it needs to be done is the true freedom in life. Freedom comes not from the absence of restraint but from the presence of discipline. When we are on the spot, when we find our-selves in the midst of a crisis, it is too late. Training in the Spiritual Disciplines is the God-ordained means for forming and transforming the human personal-ity so that when we are in a crisis we can be "response-able"—able to respond appropriately.

EXPERIENCING THE GRACE OF GOD:
THE EFFORT

It is vitally important for us to see all this spiritual training in the context of the work and action of God's grace. As the great apostle Paul reminds us, "It is God who is at work in you, enabling you both to will and to work for his good pleasure" (Phil 2:13). This, you see, is no "works righteousness," as it is sometimes called. Even our desire for this "with-God" kind of life is an action of grace; it is "prevenient grace," as the theologians say. You see, we are not just saved by grace, we live by grace. We pray by grace and fast by grace and study by grace and serve by grace and worship by grace. *All the disciplines are perme-ated by the enabling grace of God.*

But do not misunderstand—there *are* things for us to do. Daily. Grace never means inaction or total passivity. In ordinary life we will encounter many moments of decision when we must engage the will, saying "Yes!" to God's will and to God's way, as the People of God have done throughout history.

The opposite of grace is works, not effort. "Works" have to do with earning, and there simply is nothing any of us can do to earn God's love or acceptance. And, of course, we don't have to. God already loves us utterly and perfectly, and our complete acceptance is the free gift of God through Jesus Christ our Lord. In God's amazing grace, we live and move and have our being. But if we ever hope to "grow in grace," we will find ourselves engaging in effort of the most strenuous kind. As Jesus says, we are to "*strive* to enter through the narrow door" (Luke 13:24, emphasis added). And Peter urges us to "make every *effort* to support your faith with goodness, and goodness with knowledge, and knowledge with self-control, and self-control with endurance, and endurance with godliness, and godliness with mutual affection, and mutual affection with love" (2 Pet 1:5–7, emphasis added). It is this formation—indeed transformation—that we all desire.

TRAVELING WITH THE PEOPLE OF GOD: THE JOURNEY

The luminaries who walk across the pages of our Bible not only practiced the various and sundry Spiritual Disciplines that formed—indeed transformed—them into Christlikeness, but did so while on a journey. The Bible records their lives as they traveled from the Garden of Eden to Canaan to Egypt to the Promised Land to Babylon and back. Then Jesus instructed the People of God to be his witnesses "to the ends of the earth" (Acts 1:8c), until they arrive at their final destination, "a new heaven and new earth" (Rev 21:1). During their travels God made himself known in various ways to the People of God wherever they were and whatever their social situation. They reacted to God's initiatives in many ways, sometimes rejoicing, at other times rebelling. This journey has been identified by the general editors of *The Renovaré Spiritual Formation Bible* as fifteen expressions of the with-God life (see the following chart). The book you hold in your hand illuminates one dimension, The People of God with Immanuel. We hope it will help you understand how God has been with his people through the ages and continues to be with us today in our journey toward "the city that has foundations, whose architect and builder is God" (Heb 11:10).

THE PEOPLE OF GOD AND THE WITH-GOD LIFE*

Stage of Formation	Scriptures	God's Action	Human Reaction
I. The People of God in Individual Communion	Genesis 1–11**	Creates, instructs, steward of a good creation, banishes, destroys, restores	Disobey, rebel, sacrifice, murder, repent, obey
II. The People of God Become a Family	Genesis 12–50	Gives promise and establishes Abrahamic covenant, makes a great people	Faith, wrestle with God, persevere
III. The People of God in Exodus	Exodus, Leviticus, Numbers, Deuteronomy	Extends mercy, grace, and deliverance from exile; delivers the Mosaic covenant/law	Obey and disobey, develop a distinctive form of ritual
IV. The People of God in the Promised Land	Joshua, Judges, Ruth, 1 Samuel 1–12	Establishes a theocracy, bequeaths the Promised Land	Inhabit the Promised Land, accept judges as mediators
V. The People of God as a Nation	1 Samuel 13–31 & 2 Samuel, 1 & 2 Kings, 1 & 2 Chronicles, 1 Esdras 1	Permits the monarchy, exalts good kings, uses secular nations for blessing	Embrace the monarchy
VI. The People of God in Travail	Job, Psalms of Lament, Ecclesiastes, Lamentations, Tobit	Permits tribulation, allows suffering to strengthen faith	Complain yet remain faithful
VII. The People of God in Prayer and Worship	Psalms, Psalm 151	Establishes liturgical worship	Praise, prayer
VIII. The People of God in Daily Life	Proverbs, Ecclesiastes, Song of Solomon, Wisdom of Solomon, The Wisdom of Jesus Son of Sirach (Ecclesiasticus)	Gives precepts for living in community	Teachable, learning, treasure beautiful words and artistic expression
IX. The People of God in Rebellion	1 Kings 12–2 Kings 25:10, 2 Chronicles 10–36:19, Isaiah, Jeremiah 1–36, Hosea, Joel, Amos, Jonah, Micah, Nahum, Habakkuk, Zephaniah, Judith, Prayer of Manasseh	Proclaims prophetic judgment and redemption, reveals his rule over all nations, promises Immanuel, uses secular nations to bring judgment	Disbelieve and reject, believe false prophets, a faithful remnant emerges
X. The People of God in Exile	2 Kings 25:11–30, 2 Chronicles 36:20–23, Jeremiah 37–52, Lamentations, Ezekiel, Daniel, Obadiah, Baruch, Letter of Jeremiah, Additions to Daniel	Judges, yet remains faithful to covenant promises	Mourn, survive, long for Jerusalem, stand for God without institutions
XI. The People of God in Restoration	Ezra, Nehemiah, Esther, Daniel, Haggai, Zechariah, Malachi, Additions to Esther, 1 Esdras 2–9, & 2 Esdras, 1, 2, 3, & 4 Maccabees, Tobit, Additions to Daniel	Regathers and redeems, restructures social life	Return, obey, rebuild, worship, pursue Messianic figure, compile Septuagint
XII. The People of God with Immanuel	Matthew, Mark, Luke, John	Sends the Son and acts with the Son	Hear and follow, resist and reject
XIII. The People of God in Mission	Acts	Sends the Holy Spirit and creates the Church	Believe and proclaim, disbelieve and persecute
XIV. The People of God in Community	Romans, 1 & 2 Corinthians, Galatians, Ephesians, Philippians, Colossians, 1 & 2 Thessalonians, 1 & 2 Timothy, Titus, Philemon, Hebrews, James, 1 & 2 Peter, 1, 2, & 3 John, Jude	Builds, nurtures, and mobilizes the Church	Become disciples of Jesus Christ and make disciples to the ends of the earth
XV. The People of God into Eternity	Revelation	Reveals infinite progress toward infinite good	Worship and praise, creativity that magnifies God

* Text taken from *The Renovaré Spiritual Formation Bible.*
** Books are placed into categories by content, not by date of composition or type of literature.

Type of Mediation	Locus of Mediation	Social Context	Central Individual(s)	Key Spiritual Disciplines
Face-to-face	Garden, field, Noah's ark	Individuals	Adam, Eve, Enoch, Noah	Practicing the Presence, confession, sacrifice, obedience/submission
Through the family	Tent, desert, jail	Extended families and nomadic clans	Abraham and Sarah, Isaac, Jacob, Joseph	Pilgrimage, sacrifice, chastity
Through God's terrifying acts and the law	Ark of the covenant, tabernacle	Nomadic tribes	Moses	Submission, silence, simplicity, worship
Through the conquest and learning to act with God	Shiloh, Bethel	An ethnic people with fluid leadership	Joshua, Deborah, Ruth, Samson, Gideon, Samuel	Guidance, radical obedience/submission, secrecy
Through the king, prophets, priests, and sacrifices	Altars, consecrated places, first (Solomonic) Temple	Political nation on the world stage	Saul, David, Hezekiah, Elijah, Elisha	Worship, prayer
Through suffering and the disappointments of life	Ash heap, hard circumstances of life	Individual	Job, Israel as the suffering servant	Fasting, solitude, silence, submission, service, celebration
Through song, prayer, worship	Jerusalem, flowering of individual experience	Nation	David	Prayer, worship, confession, celebration, meditation
Through wisdom	Temple, in the gate, home	Nation triumphant	Solomon	Study, guidance, celebration, meditation
Through the prophets and repression by the Gentiles	High places, Temple desecrated and destroyed	Nation under siege and dispersed	Isaiah, Hosea, Amos	Fasting, repentance, obedience/submission, solitude, silence, the law internalized
Through punishment, being a blessing to their captors	Babylon, anyplace, anytime	Ethnics abroad without a political homeland	Ezekiel, Jeremiah	Detachment, fasting, simplicity, prayer, silence, service
Through repentance, service, synagogue study	Rebuilt Temple, synagogue	Remnant on the international scene, ethnics in the leadership of other nations	Ezra, Cyrus the Persian, Nehemiah, Maccabees, Essenes, John the Baptist	Pilgrimage, confession, worship, study, service
Through the Incarnate Word and the living presence of the kingdom	Temple and synagogue, boats and hillsides, gatherings of disciples	Small groups, disciples, apostles, hostile critics	Jesus Christ Incarnate	Celebration, study, pilgrimage, submission, prayer, sacrifice, obedience, confession
Through the Holy Spirit, persecution, and martyrdom	Temple, synagogue, schools, riversides, public square	Jew, Gentile, house churches, abandonment of social strata	Peter, Paul	Speaking and hearing the word, sacrifice, guidance, generosity/service, fasting, prayer
In one another, through Scripture, teaching, preaching, prophetic utterance, pastoral care, the Holy Spirit, the sacraments	Gathered community	Community redefined by the Body of Christ, decadent Greco-Roman culture	Peter, Paul, John	Prayer, study, accountability/submission, fellowship
Throughout the cosmos	Focused in the New Jerusalem and extending throughout the cosmos	The Trinity and its community	God the Father, Son, and Holy Spirit; apostles, prophets	Living beyond disciplines

LEARNING FROM JESUS: AN OVERVIEW

As God incarnate, God in the flesh, Jesus offered a previously unknown personal knowledge of God and fellowship with him. In addition, Jesus's birth, life, death, and resurrection became the foundation of Christian belief and practice. Jesus Christ is the central figure in our lives as Christians. For us to be near to the Father as Jesus was near to the Father, we need to be near Jesus. As we come closer to him, Jesus Christ informs and transforms us.

In a small book like this one, we cannot hope to encompass all of Jesus's life, his teachings, and their significance. We have attempted to look at who Jesus is, how he interacted with those around him, and some of his teachings, while always asking the question: What does this mean for our spiritual formation, for our growth into Christlikeness? For it is in Jesus that this concept of spiritual formation is illuminated. As *The Renovaré Spiritual Formation Bible* states, "At last it becomes absolutely clear what 'spiritual formation' is all about: disciples are to teach 'them everything that I have commanded you' (Matt 28:20). Obedience means to bring our inner person into such a transformed condition that the deeds of Christ naturally arise out of it. It is not to focus on the actions themselves, for that way leads to deadly legalism, and surely we have had enough of that already. Instead Christian spiritual formation focuses on becoming a 'good tree' with the full assurance that 'no good tree bears bad fruit' (Luke 6:43). The end result of such a process is a natural and 'automatic' obedience to Christ and his way."[1]

By studying Jesus's life and words, while seeking to become ever more obedient and guarding against legalism, we see that he teaches that the kingdom of God is available to us all and that we can be part of it right now. By taking on the mantle of flesh, Jesus teaches us that the physical—our bodies, our world—is beautiful and holy. Furthermore, Jesus's life shows us that we are engaging in discipleship at all times—in our workplace and in our family life as well as when we are actively engaged in religious rituals or engrossed in prayer.

Even better, Jesus himself continues to teach us. He has not contracted laryngitis. His voice is not hard to hear. His vocabulary is not difficult to understand. He is the good shepherd, and his sheep do hear his voice. He guides his people. He corrects his people. He forgives his people. He instructs his people. He oversees his people. He empowers his people.

Are you ready to learn from Jesus?

EXPECTING
THE MESSIAH

1

DEVOTIONAL READING

PHILIP YANCEY, *The Jesus I Never Knew*

It would be impossible to exaggerate the import of the word *Messiah* among faithful Jews. The Dead Sea Scrolls discovered in 1947 confirm that the Qumran community imminently expected a Messiah-like figure, setting aside an empty seat for him each day at the sacred meal. Audacious as it may be to dream that a tiny province wedged in among great powers would produce a worldwide ruler, nonetheless Jews believed just that. They staked their future on a king who would lead their nation back to glory.

During Jesus' lifetime, revolt was in the air. Pseudo-messiahs periodically emerged to lead rebellions, only to be crushed in ruthless crackdowns. To take just one example, a prophet known as "the Egyptian" attracted multitudes into the wilderness where he proclaimed that at his command the walls of Jerusalem would fall; the Roman governor sent a detachment of soldiers after them and killed four thousand of the rebels.

When another report spread that the long-awaited prophet had turned up in the desert, crowds flocked to see the wild man dressed in camel skin. "I am not the Christ [Messiah]," insisted John the Baptist, who then proceeded to raise hopes even higher by speaking in exalted terms of one who would soon appear. John's question of Jesus, "Are you the one who was to come, or shall we expect someone else?" was in a real sense the question of the age, whispered everywhere.

Every Hebrew prophet had taught that someday God would install his kingdom on earth, and that is why rumors about the "Son of David" so inflamed Jewish hopes. God would prove in person that he had not forsaken them. He would, as Isaiah had cried, "rend the heavens and

It is helpful for everyone to read the Devotional and Scripture Readings and do the My Life with God Exercise before the meeting. Begin the meeting with silent prayer, then move directly to Reflecting on My Life with God below.

come down, that the mountains would tremble before you!... come down to cause the nations to quake before you."

But let us be honest. When the one John pointed to arrived on the scene, neither the mountains trembled nor the nations quaked. Jesus did not come close to satisfying the lavish hopes of the Jews. The opposite happened: within a generation Roman soldiers razed Jerusalem to the ground.[1]

MY LIFE WITH GOD EXERCISE

Philip Yancey, a Christian, writes that Jesus didn't fulfill the "lavish hopes" of the Jews. As a way to understand the religious and political milieu into which Jesus was born, we will try to examine the Jewish expectations for the Messiah. The word *Messiah* means simply "anointed one." We find the word applied in Scripture to kings of Israel, such as Saul, David, and Solomon. But after the Davidic line was broken and the nation of Israel exiled into Assyrian and Babylonian captivity, the prophets of the day, Isaiah and Jeremiah, and others, began to speak of a time when God would restore his people through a king in the line of David. In the book of Daniel, we find the first specific mention of a "Messiah" or "anointed prince" (9:25) associated with this expected restoration. As Yancey writes, by the time of Jesus, not only were the Jewish people expecting the Messiah to come at any moment, but they had very high expectations for what this Messiah was to accomplish. According to Rabbi Joseph Telushkin, the Jewish people expect the Messiah to "be a descendant of King David, gain sovereignty over the land of Israel, gather the Jews there from the four corners of the earth, restore them to full observance of Torah law, and, as a grand finale, bring peace to the whole world."[2]

To better familiarize ourselves with the Messiah expected by the Jews, we will read some of the Scriptures commonly interpreted as predicting the coming of the Messiah. Over the next week, read these Scriptures and consider how they support Rabbi Telushkin's five criteria: Isaiah 2:2–4; 9:6–7; 11:1–12; 16:4b–5; 22:22–23; 27:12–13; 52:13; 56:8; 60:4–5; 61:4–6; Jeremiah 23:5–8; 31:31–34; 33:14–17; Micah 5:2–5a; Zechariah 9:9–10. Also look for additional characteristics the Messiah is to have. It might be helpful to list the five criteria as column heads on a notepad and copy down phrases or chapter and verse references for the various points. Do the same for any additional characteristics of the Messiah that you find in the Scripture passages.

LEARNING FROM JESUS

What did you learn about the kind of Messiah the Jews expect? How did this fit with your own ideas about Jesus?

REFLECTING ON MY LIFE WITH GOD Allow each member a few moments to answer this question.

➤ **SCRIPTURE READING:** LUKE 3:1–17

✍ After everyone has had a chance to respond to the question, ask a member to read this passage from Scripture.

In the fifteenth year of the reign of Emperor Tiberius, when Pontius Pilate was governor of Judea, and Herod was ruler of Galilee, and his brother Philip ruler of the region of Ituraea and Trachonitis, and Lysanias ruler of Abilene, during the high priesthood of Annas and Caiaphas, the word of God came to John son of Zechariah in the wilderness. He went into all the region around the Jordan, proclaiming a baptism of repentance for the forgiveness of sins, as it is written in the book of the words of the prophet Isaiah,

> "The voice of one crying out in the wilderness:
> 'Prepare the way of the Lord, make his paths straight.
> Every valley shall be filled,
>   and every mountain and hill shall be made low,
> and the crooked shall be made straight,
>   and the rough ways made smooth;
> and all flesh shall see the salvation of God.'"

John said to the crowds that came out to be baptized by him, "You brood of vipers! Who warned you to flee from the wrath to come? Bear fruits worthy of repentance. Do not begin to say to yourselves, 'We have Abraham as our ancestor'; for I tell you, God is able from these stones to raise up children to Abraham. Even now the ax is lying at the root of the trees; every tree therefore that does not bear good fruit is cut down and thrown into the fire."

And the crowds asked him, "What then should we do?" In reply he said to them, "Whoever has two coats must share with anyone who has none; and whoever has food must do likewise." Even tax collectors came to be baptized, and they asked him, "Teacher, what should we do?" He said to them, "Collect no more than the amount prescribed for you." Soldiers also asked him, "And we, what should we do?" He said to them, "Do not extort money from anyone by threats or false accusation, and be satisfied with your wages."

As the people were filled with expectation, and all were questioning in their hearts concerning John, whether he might be the Messiah, John answered all of them by saying, "I baptize you with water; but one who is more powerful than I is coming; I am not worthy to untie the thong of his sandals. He will baptize you with the Holy Spirit and fire. His winnowing fork is in his hand, to clear his threshing floor and to gather the wheat into his granary; but the chaff he will burn with unquenchable fire."

REFLECTION QUESTION
Allow each person a few moments to respond to this question.

What kind of Messiah did John the Baptist announce? Keeping in mind the Devotional Reading, how is the Messiah the Jews are expecting different from the Messiah that John the Baptist announced? How are they similar?

▶▶ GETTING THE PICTURE

✍ After a brief discussion, choose one person to read this section.

At the time of John the Baptist, expectations for the Messiah are high. As we read in the Devotional Reading by Philip Yancey, Jews are looking for the Messiah in various charismatic figures of the times. At first they think John the Baptist might be the Messiah, but John clarifies that he is the latest of the long line of prophets who have proclaimed the living word of God, the *debar Yahweh,* to kings and commoners alike since Israel's beginnings as a nation. These prophets had been the first to announce the coming of the Messiah of whom John speaks. Before Assyria invaded and conquered the Northern Kingdom, Israel, in 720 BC, and Babylon the Southern Kingdom, Judah, in 586 BC, the prophets of God had warned that the nation would be overrun and its inhabitants sent into exile if they continued to worship false gods and practice injustice. For the most part, their warnings went unheeded, but the people did remember that many times the warnings were linked to a promise of future redemption by an anointed figure, a Messiah.

After the Jews lost their national independence, the writings of the literary prophets became popular among Jews living in Palestine and throughout the diaspora, particularly those writings that predicted that a Messiah would restore the Jewish nation and Temple to their former glory. Starting in the time of the last biblical prophet (around 400 BC), political changes such as wars, migrations of people, invasions, and the rise and fall of nations impacted the scattered Jewish communities and stimulated speculation about the coming Messiah.

By Jesus's time, several schools of Messianic thought and expectations have emerged. Within the five general criteria set out by Rabbi Telushkin (the Messiah would "be a descendant of King David, gain sovereignty over the land of Israel, gather the Jews there from the four corners of the earth, restore them to full observance of Torah law, and bring peace to the whole world"),[3] Jewish groups focus on the aspects of the Messiah that most closely match their beliefs. The Sadducees, the theological conservatives of the day, conform to the dominant non-Jewish cultures and place a high value on social stability. Their primary concern is maintaining national Jewish religious ritual despite Roman occupation. When they do turn to thoughts of a Messiah, they expect him to be one of their contemporaries. Some Sadducees even think Herod might be the Messiah. One school of Pharisees include the theological legalists who urge everyone to follow to the letter their interpretation of the law of Moses. Their Messiah would lead this charge. Two other influential groups—the Zealots and the Essenes—take opposite approaches. The Zealots want to forcefully remove the Romans from power and install a Messiah; the Essenes retreat into the desert, waiting for two Messiahs to come. In this charged atmosphere of conflicting expectations, John the Baptist proclaims that the Messiah has arrived.

▶▶▶ GOING DEEPER

John the Baptist, who continued Israel's rich prophetic tradition, had a ready-made audience. And in proclaiming that he was not the Messiah but that the Messiah was coming, he captured the attention of many who would otherwise have thought that he was just a wild man who lived in the desert, wore camel hair, and ate locusts and honey. John's message prepared the way for a Messiah who would not conform to the expectations of the people. Whereas the Sadducees were looking for a Messiah who would not upset the social order, John proclaimed an upside-down kingdom that challenged the status quo, changing the categories of rich and poor. Whereas the Pharisees were looking for a Messiah who would bring all Jews to full observance of the law, John's words were the first hint that Jesus would redefine the law. Whereas the Zealots were looking for a Messiah who would throw off the yoke of Roman occupation, John's words mentioned nothing about political power. Whereas the Essenes were looking for a Messiah who would approve their commitment to living apart from society and initiate an apocalyptic ending to human history, John instead called them to repentance, baptism, and full engagement with the world.

John the Baptist turned the expectations for a Messiah upside down, while teaching us about the importance of sin and repentance. Sin must be called sin. John the Baptist didn't soften his words to keep from

⌇ Have another member read this section.

hurting someone's feelings. He was particularly frank with the Pharisees and Sadducees (see Matt 3:7–9). Thus we must be perfectly honest with ourselves in dealing with the sin in our lives.

John also emphasized that repentance is necessary. The type of repentance to which John the Baptist called people differed from the Old Testament tradition, which centered around a liturgy in which the assembly or nation as a whole fasted, lamented, and confessed their sin. John's call to repentance required an interior conversion in which the person showed kindness, humility, and a commitment to justice. John called his listeners to an authentic change of heart that manifested itself in baptism. In asking for repentance, John, and later Jesus, called individuals to reconsider their priorities and ways of thinking about how to live in the world, and to adjust their lives accordingly. That call to repentance was intimately connected to the arrival of the kingdom of God and the coming of the Messiah.

John the Baptist taught that a genuine conversion of the heart will express itself in outward actions. He cited several things that we will do when our heart has changed: share our clothing and food with those in need, be honest in our monetary transactions, refrain from extortion, tell the truth, and be content with our wages (in other words, avoid greed). These are only some examples of the many ways that our actions change when we experience a truly converted heart.

Finally, our religious heritage will not put or keep us in right relationship with God. The Sadducees relied on their status as children of Abraham, and the Pharisees relied on their adherence to the Mosaic law for their relationship with God. Although that was good, it was not enough. While focusing on tracing their ancestry and observing the teeniest commands, they forgot the spirit of the law, which is to "love the Lord your God with all your heart, and with all your soul, and with all your mind" and "love your neighbor as yourself" (Matt 22:37, 39).

REFLECTION QUESTION
Allow each person a few moments to respond.

What is the most compelling part of John the Baptist's message? The most countercultural for us?

▶▶▶ POINTING TO GOD

🕊 Choose one member to read this section.

Dietrich Bonhoeffer, the German theologian and martyr, who is best known for his passionate opposition to the Nazi regime in Germany, has often been compared to John the Baptist. Bonhoeffer, a well-known teacher, spoke out from the pulpit and on the radio against the racist actions of Hitler's government. He argued that the church had a responsibility to question and even reproach governmental leadership. Just as John the Baptist preached to a world that was expecting a very different type of Messiah, Bonhoeffer confronted a church, and indeed a German nation, that held a very different idea of what it was to be a Christian in the face of the ethnic discrimination and genocidal practices of the Nazi regime.

Bonhoeffer was surrounded by groups that bore a surprising similarity to the Jewish leaders of Jesus's time. The German Evangelical Church split into two branches—the Reich Church, made up of "German Christians" who supported Hitler and had passed the Aryan Clause as church policy for ministers, and the Confessing Church, which denounced the Aryan Clause and other Nazi policies as un-Christlike. Like the Sadducees, members of the Reich Church were all too eager to fall in line with the policies of the ruling party so as to have their share of temporal power. But as the Nazis became more firmly entrenched in German society, even many members of the Confessing Church, like the Pharisees, concerned about keeping their hands clean in this messy situation, refused to speak out against the injustices done to their fellow Germans. Bonhoeffer, however, continued to speak out, especially against those Christians who claimed the Jews deserved mistreatment because they had killed Jesus. In 1939 Bonhoeffer left the ever-worsening situation in Germany for a teaching position at Union Theological Seminary in New York City, but soon decided to return to Germany. He believed that those Germans who chose to leave Germany, like the Essenes who fled to the desert, were making a grave mistake not working for God within their own society. As Bonhoeffer wrote in a goodbye letter to his Union Seminary colleague Reinhold Niebuhr, "I have made a mistake in coming to America. I must live through this difficult period of our national history with the Christian people of Germany. I will have no right to participate in the reconstruction of Christian life in Germany after the war if I do not share the trials of this time with my people."[4]

Back in Germany Bonhoeffer became a double agent and, while ostensibly working for the government, joined a group of conspirators trying to overthrow the government. This group was much like the Zealots of John the Baptist's day in its commitment to overcome the ruling power by any means necessary, but Bonhoeffer decided that siding with this group was the lesser evil. Their attempt to assassinate Hitler failed, and Bonhoeffer was arrested and put to death, just weeks before the end of World War II.[5]

Like John the Baptist, Bonhoeffer faced unexpected challenges and difficulties in his life. Their lives bore out a lesson Jesus taught us through his own life: God's ways are surprising and unpredictable, and when we choose to follow him our lives bear the same characteristics. As *The Renovaré Spiritual Formation Bible* puts it, "God's coming in the person of Jesus Christ, from the babe and the carpenter to the cross and the resurrection, was totally unexpected and incomprehensible to human ways of thinking. This reminds us that God can never be tamed or domesticated. In fact, we need to be immediately suspicious of proposals and arrangements that make perfect human sense."[6]

John the Baptist and Bonhoeffer confronted the prevailing ideas of their time and suffered for it. Like John the Baptist, Bonhoeffer could be considered a failure: the assassination he planned with other Christians failed, he was unable to convince the Confessing Church to speak out against Hitler, and he was eventually executed for his role in the assassination plot.[7] Yet Bonhoeffer's life story and his writings have challenged and inspired countless Christians, both during and after his life. In killing him, the Nazi regime did not silence his powerful witness but strengthened it.

▶▶▶▶▶ GOING FORWARD

Have another person read this section.

Jesus was not accepted as the Messiah by many people of his time because he simply wasn't the kind of messiah they had been conditioned to expect. He was more humble than kingly, he advocated practicing the spirit of the law rather than the letter, he confronted the culture rather than fleeing it, and perhaps most difficult to accept, he did not attempt to destroy Israel's enemies and bring power and glory to her people. Instead he—and John the Baptist before him—asked the Jews to repent of their sins and to practice justice, humility, and kindness toward others. What a bitter pill to swallow.

We Christians often have an equally hard time with this aspect of Jesus. We prefer to think of him as first our buddy, the one who is on our side only, and second as our judge and warrior, who will exact revenge on the rest of the world when the time is right. Our ideas are no less wrong, no less incomplete, than those of the Pharisees, Sadducees, Zealots, and Essenes of Jesus's time. Each group made the mistake of focusing on one aspect of the Messiah—advocating social stability, teaching adherence to the law, challenging the political structure, retreating from the world—and placing too much emphasis upon this one aspect, distorting the rest of the picture. Living as we do in a world distorted by sin, none of us can be too smug about our knowledge of Jesus or feel that we have a lock on the truth. Jesus was constantly challenging the expectations of those around him. Just as none of us fully understands everything about Jesus, our Messiah, none of us can ignore his call to repent, to recognize and confess our sins and work to do better. His call can be hard to hear. It can be even more difficult to follow. As with Bonhoeffer, it may lead us down a road of pain and suffering, even death. Yet we do not go down that path alone. Jesus has gone before us.

Like the religious leaders of Jesus's time, we often cling to one idea or one part of Jesus's teachings that fits our own beliefs and exalt this one aspect above all others, distorting the rest of the picture and ignoring teachings we find less palatable. Think about your expectations of Jesus. Which characteristics or teachings of Jesus do you tend to emphasize? What characteristics or teachings do you tend to downplay?

REFLECTION QUESTION
Again, allow each member a few moments to answer this question.

This concludes our look at expectations of the Messiah. In the next chapter we will turn our attention to another avenue of learning from Jesus—Jesus as the Word become flesh.

✍ After everyone has had a chance to respond, the leader reads this paragraph.

✍ **Allow some time for members to encourage one another to read the Devotional and Scripture Readings and do the exercise in the following chapter before the next meeting.** Then invite the members to be silent for a few moments before leading them in reading the Closing Prayer aloud together.

CLOSING PRAYER

The Lord is my shepherd, I shall not want.
    He makes me lie down in green pastures;
he leads me beside still waters;
    he restores my soul.
He leads me in right paths
    for his name's sake.

Even though I walk through the darkest valley,
    I fear no evil;
for you are with me;
    your rod and your staff—
    they comfort me.

You prepare a table before me
    in the presence of my enemies;
you anoint my head with oil;
    my cup overflows.

At the end of the Closing Prayer, the leader asks for a volunteer to lead the next meeting.

Surely goodness and mercy shall follow me
all the days of my life,
and I shall dwell in the house of the LORD
my whole life long. (PS 23)

TAKING IT FURTHER

ADDITIONAL EXERCISES

- You are almost certainly familiar with "Oh, Come, Oh, Come, Emmanuel," but often we sing familiar songs without really paying attention to the words. Read or sing the following verses in light of the expectations of the Messiah we discussed in this chapter. Did Jesus fulfill all these expectations?

Oh, come, oh, come, Emmanuel,
And ransom captive Israel,
That mourns in lonely exile here
Until the Son of God appear.

Refrain: Rejoice! Rejoice! Emmanuel
Shall come to you, O Israel.

Oh, come, oh, come, great Lord of might,
Who to your tribes on Sinai's height
In ancient times once gave the law
In cloud, and majesty, and awe. *Refrain*

Oh, come, strong Branch of Jesse, free
Your own from Satan's tyranny;
From depths of hell your people save
And give them vict'ry o'er the grave. *Refrain*

Oh, come, blest Dayspring, come and cheer
Our spirits by your advent here;
Dispense the gloomy clouds of night,
and death's dark shadows put to flight. *Refrain*

Oh, come, O Key of David, come,
and open wide our heav'nly home;
Make safe the way that leads on high,
And close the path to misery. *Refrain*[8]

- To learn more about the Israelite prophetic tradition, watch the movie *Jeremiah* (Vidmark/Trimark, 2000). Another good resource is *In the Footsteps of Alexander* (Paramount Home Video, 2004), which depicts some of the events that shaped the culture of Jesus's time.

ADDITIONAL RESOURCES

Bonhoeffer, Dietrich. *A Testament to Freedom*. Edited by Geffrey B. Kelly and F. Burton Nelson. San Francisco: HarperSanFrancisco, 1990, 1995.

Telushkin, Joseph. *Jewish Literacy*. New York: William Morrow, 1991.

Yancey, Philip. *The Jesus I Never Knew*. Grand Rapids, MI: Zondervan, 1995.

ADDITIONAL REFLECTION QUESTIONS

When has an event or person in your life failed to meet your expectations? What was your reaction?

How do you think John the Baptist's message would be received today? What parts do you find particularly compelling for today's world?

Consider the society at large or your particular social circles in terms of dominant groups like the Sadducees, Pharisees, Zealots, and Essenes of Jesus's time. What kind of messiah are the influential groups in your life pointing to?

AND THE WORD BECAME FLESH ...

2

DEVOTIONAL READING

SAINT AUGUSTINE, *On the Trinity*

If the Son is said to be sent by the Father, . . . this does not in any manner hinder us from believing the Son to be equal, and consubstantial, and co-eternal with the Father, and yet to have been sent as Son by the Father. Not because the one is greater, the other less; but because the one is Father, the other Son; the one begetter, the other begotten; the one, He from whom He is who is sent; the other, He who is from Him who sends. For the Son is from the Father, not the Father from the Son. And according to this manner we can now understand that the Son is not only said to have been sent because "the Word was made flesh" (John i.3, 18, 14), but therefore sent that the Word might be made flesh, and that He might perform through His bodily presence those things which were written; that is, that not only is He understood to have been sent as man, which the Word was made but the Word, too, was sent that it might be made man; because He was not sent in respect to any inequality of power, or substance, or anything that in Him was not equal to the Father; but in respect to this, that the Son is from the Father, not the Father from the Son; for the Son is the Word of the Father, which is also called His wisdom. . . .

But when the Son of God was made manifest in the flesh, He was sent into this world in the fullness of time, made of a woman. "For after that, in the wisdom of God, the world by wisdom knew not God" (since "the light shineth in darkness, and the darkness comprehended it not"), it "pleased God by the foolishness of preaching to save them that believe" (1 Cor. i.21) and that the Word should be made flesh, and dwell among us (John i.5, 14). . . .

It is helpful for everyone to read the Devotional and Scripture Readings and do the My Life with God Exercise before the meeting. Begin the meeting with silent prayer, then move directly to Reflecting on My Life with God below.

As, therefore, the Father begat, the Son is begotten; so the Father sent, the Son was sent. But in like manner as He who begat and He who was begotten, so both He who sent and He who was sent, are one, since the Father and the Son are one (John x.30). So also the Holy Spirit is one with them, since these three are one. For as to be born, in respect to the Son, means to be from the Father; so to be sent, in respect to the Son, means to be known to be from the Father. And as to be the gift of God in respect to the Holy Spirit, means to proceed from the Father; so to be sent, is to be known to proceed from the Father. Neither can we say that the Holy Spirit does not also proceed from the Son, for the same Spirit is not without reason said to be the Spirit both of the Father and of the Son. Nor do I see what else He intended to signify, when He breathed on the face of the disciples, and said, "Receive ye the Holy Ghost" (John xx.22). For that bodily breathing, proceeding from the body with the feeling of bodily touching, was not the substance of the Holy Spirit, but a declaration by a fitting sign, that the Holy Spirit proceeds not only from the Father, but also from the Son. For the veriest of madmen would not say, that it was one Spirit which He gave when He breathed on them, and another which He sent after his ascension (Acts ii.1–4). For the Spirit of God is one, the Spirit of the Father and of the Son, the Holy Spirit, who worketh all in all.[1]

MY LIFE WITH GOD EXERCISE

Of all the writings on the Trinity, Saint Augustine's is likely the most well known. At the same time, *On the Trinity* is one of the hardest to read and understand. For all its difficulty, it is helpful to be familiar with this excerpt from Augustine's work, which explains the relationship of God the Father, God the Son, and God the Holy Spirit.

To help get beyond the excerpt's archaic language to its life-giving concept of the Trinity, here is our suggestion: read the excerpt as many times as you can. As you are reading, pause over any phrase or sentence you don't understand and ask God to give you the wisdom to reveal its meaning to your mind and heart. Then read it again. And again. And again if you have to.

After you have read the piece several times, try to paraphrase it. Don't worry about length or polish; just try to capture the essence of the passage. Please don't get discouraged as you are trying to understand what Saint Augustine writes; the brightest scholars have difficulty, too. If you find you absolutely can't understand it, fine. We don't have to understand obscure writings in order to learn from Jesus. But remember: many people approach pieces like these with a "nothing ventured, nothing gained" attitude. We hope you can do the same.

What does Augustine teach about the relationship between God the Father, God the Son, and God the Holy Spirit? How does that affect your view of the Trinity? Did you learn more after spending additional time with the excerpt?

REFLECTING ON MY LIFE WITH GOD
Allow each member a few moments to answer this question.

➤ SCRIPTURE READING: JOHN 1:1–18

✍ After everyone has had a chance to respond, to the question, ask a member to read this passage from Scripture.

In the beginning was the Word, and the Word was with God, and the Word was God. He was in the beginning with God. All things came into being through him, and without him not one thing came into being. What has come into being in him was life, and the life was the light of all people. The light shines in the darkness, and the darkness did not overcome it.

There was a man sent from God, whose name was John. He came as a witness to testify to the light, so that all might believe through him. He himself was not the light, but he came to testify to the light. The true light, which enlightens everyone, was coming into the world.

He was in the world, and the world came into being through him; yet the world did not know him. He came to what was his own, and his own people did not accept him. But to all who received him, who believed in his name, he gave power to become children of God, who were born, not of blood or of the will of the flesh or of the will of man, but of God.

And the Word became flesh and lived among us, and we have seen his glory, the glory as of a father's only son, full of grace and truth. (John testified to him and cried out, "This was he of whom I said, 'He who comes after me ranks ahead of me because he was before me.'") From his fullness we have all received, grace upon grace. The law indeed was given through Moses; grace and truth came through Jesus Christ. No one has ever seen God. It is God the only Son, who is close to the Father's heart, who had made him known.

REFLECTION QUESTION
Allow each person a few
moments to respond to
this question.

What does this passage from John add to your understanding about the Trinity? Does it support or challenge the view of the Trinity presented in the Devotional Reading?

▶▶ GETTING THE PICTURE

These eighteen verses, commonly known as the prologue to the book of John, succinctly, elegantly, powerfully explain the origin of the Word, the *Logos*. John's opening sentence, "In the beginning was the Word (*Logos*)," hearkens back to memories of God speaking the universe into being, God calling Abraham to leave his homeland, or Isaac uttering a blessing over Jacob instead of Esau. As these examples indicate, words had great power in the Jewish world. Once a word was spoken, the event was happening. Words couldn't be taken back. "In the beginning was the Word (*Logos*)" connected with the Jewish mind on a deep level.

Not only did *Logos* resonate deeply with Jews, but it also had special meaning for Gentiles. In the inquisitive, sophisticated world of Greek philosophical thought, *Logos* was first viewed as the Reason of God. Later the Stoics considered it to be the mind of God, which was "the eternal principle of order in the universe, that which makes the chaos of the world a cosmos."[2]

Thus these two widely divergent cultures—Jewish and Greek—are drawn into John's simple, single concept, which introduces the second person of the Trinity, Jesus Christ. Jesus Christ is the Word of God made flesh. "'The Word' and the Father are not identical, yet They are One," writes pastor Roger Fredrikson.[3] And this uncreated Word has always been, since before the beginning of the universe. Furthermore, the Word "was God." The Word, *Logos*, was, and is, divine. And intimated but not explicitly stated in the prologue to the Gospel of John, there is a third member of the Trinity, the Holy Spirit, which participates fully in the miracle in which "the Word became flesh." "The angel said to [Mary], 'The Holy Spirit will come upon you, and the power of the Most High will overshadow you; therefore the child to be born will be holy; he will be called Son of God" (Luke 1:35). So it was spoken, and so it is.

▶▶▶ GOING DEEPER

The prologue to John's Gospel is so full of teaching that applies to our spiritual formation that it is hard to pick only a few items. Therefore, we will focus our attention on those that we feel are the most important. To begin, Jesus Christ is the agent through which the whole material creation came into being. This means that Jesus Christ designed and maintains every breath of air we take, every beat of our hearts, every morsel of food we eat, every raw material we use, everything. Not one thing is excluded. All have their source in Jesus Christ.

Jesus Christ is also the source of all that is nonmaterial in our world, particularly our spiritual life. The love we have for each other and God, the compassion we feel for the sick and lost, the impulse to serve those less fortunate than ourselves, and the desire to become intimate with God all have their source in Jesus Christ. This life—this light, as John calls it—guides us and enriches us and makes us fully human. As embodied spirits we need a fellow human—we might say a spirit with a body—Jesus Christ, to show us how to live in harmony with God. The rituals and laws of the Old Testament taught God's people about God, but the people lacked a living example. Jesus was the Word who became flesh. He was made of bone and tissue and blood just like us. God took on the mantle of flesh to be our model, a teacher we could learn from and emulate.

Jesus Christ is the source of grace. This grace is not only the unmerited favor that saves us from being separated from God for eternity ("For by grace you have been saved through faith, and this is not your own doing; it is the gift of God—not the result of works, so that no one may boast" [Eph 2:8–9]), but it also gives us physical life and keeps us alive. Probably the best way to illustrate this kind of grace is by a passage from Job: "In [God's] hand is the life of every living thing and the breath of every human being" (12:10). Not only does grace give us spiritual and physical life, but we grow as a result of God's grace. Grace is God's action in our lives. We live off that action; we feed off God; we participate with God in our growth. As the apostle Peter wrote, we are to "grow in the grace and knowledge of our Lord and Savior Jesus Christ" (2 Pet 3:18).

Finally, Jesus Christ is the source of all truth. For centuries Greek philosophers from Socrates to Plato to Aristotle had been seeking the truth. The Egyptian pharaohs had been surrounded by scholars and religious priests. The search for truth in every culture was almost like the search for the fountain of youth: desired yet elusive. Truth in all its fullness arrived on earth when God was born of a virgin and grew into an adult as an ordinary human being. We have only to look at Jesus's teachings to see truth shining in them as the sun shines at midday.

REFLECTION QUESTION
Allow each person a few
moments to respond.

What does it mean for you that Jesus was the Word become flesh?

▶▶▶▶ POINTING TO GOD

✍ Choose one member
to read this section.

In spite of the statements in the Gospels and Epistles that the Godhead consists of more than one expression of divinity, it took the early church centuries to define and refine its doctrine of the Trinity. Disagreements over a number of issues, including what Jesus had accomplished and the divine and human nature of the risen Christ, precipitated the convening of seven ecumenical councils from AD 325 through 787. The first council, held in Nicea, was called primarily to debate the claims of Arius, an Alexandrian priest who had been teaching that God the Father existed before Jesus and that Jesus was subordinate to God. Another priest, Athanasius of Alexandria, argued convincingly that Jesus was fully divine, and the council determined that Jesus was "begotten not made" and was *homoousios* ("one in being" or "of one substance") with the Father. This issue was and is considered crucial because, as Athanasius pointed out, if Jesus was a creature created by God, he could not have redeemed humanity. A creature cannot be redeemed by another creature. And since Christians pray to Christ, if he is not divine then Christians are guilty of idolatry. Their discussion led to the creation of the Nicene Creed, which Christians still confess:

> We believe in one God,
>> the Father, the Almighty,
>> maker of heaven and earth,
>> of all that is, seen and unseen.

> We believe in one Lord, Jesus Christ,
>> the only Son of God,
>> eternally begotten of the Father,
>> God from God, Light from Light,
>> true God from true God,
>> begotten, not made,
>> of one Being with the Father.
>> Through him all things were made.
>> For us and for our salvation
>>> he came down from heaven:
>> by the power of the Holy Spirit
>>> he became incarnate from the Virgin Mary,
>>> and was made man.

For our sake he was crucified under Pontius Pilate;
 he suffered death and was buried.
 On the third day he rose again
  in accordance with the Scriptures;
 he ascended into heaven
  and is seated at the right hand of the Father.
He will come again in glory to judge the living and the dead,
 and his kingdom will have no end.

Six other ecumenical councils followed. The second council declared that Christ is fully human and affirmed the deity of the Holy Spirit. It was after this council that the last paragraph was added to the Nicene Creed:

We believe in the Holy Spirit, the Lord, the giver of life,
 who proceeds from the Father and the Son.
 With the Father and the Son he is worshiped and glorified.
 He has spoken through the Prophets.
 We believe in one holy catholic* and apostolic Church.
 We acknowledge one baptism for the forgiveness of sins.
 We look for the resurrection of the dead,
  and the life of the world to come. Amen.

The third council declared that Christ is a unified person and that Mary is *Theotokos*, "God-bearer." The fourth, held at Chalcedon, declared that Christ is "two natures (divine and human) in one person." The fifth reaffirmed the council at Chalcedon. The sixth declared that Christ possessed both a human will and a divine will, which function together in perfect moral harmony. And the seventh, the last true ecumenical council, affirmed that "icons and other symbols are acceptable aids to worship and devotion."[4]

▶▶▶▶▶ GOING FORWARD

The Trinity is one of the most complicated and confusing theological concepts in Christianity. For most of us, seeking to understand it is at best a struggle. It may even seem a waste of time. We might wonder what difference the theology of the Trinity really makes for our own personal relationship with God. But the truth is that doctrine and theology are

✍ Have another person read this section.

* i.e., universal.

And the Word Became Flesh . . .

important instruments of spiritual formation. We learn important lessons about God and about how we can follow him by trying our best to understand God's nature and the way he works. The more we know about God, the better we can love and enjoy him. The fact that God's being is expressed in the Father, the Son, and the Holy Spirit teaches us a fundamental truth about ourselves as human beings. We need to be not only created, but also redeemed and sanctified. These three needs of ours are beautifully met in the Trinity.

A further lesson can be learned from the fact that some aspects of the Trinity—how God is one and three at the same time—will always remain shrouded in mystery. As Ellen Charry puts it, the Trinity is "not a secret to be disclosed, a riddle to be answered or a puzzle to be solved but an enigma to be dwelt in.... This impenetrability or unknowability of God is a lesson in humility."[5] In direct contrast to secular sensibilities and their championing of the limitless bounds of human knowledge, God teaches us that we cannot and maybe should not know or control everything.[6] We can love and enjoy God even without understanding all there is to know about him.

REFLECTION QUESTION
Again, allow each member a few moments to answer this question.

How might dwelling on a theological statement such as the Nicene Creed aid in spiritual growth?

✍ After everyone has had a chance to respond, the leader reads this paragraph.

This concludes our look at Jesus as the Word become flesh as the second person of the Trinity. In the next chapter we will turn our attention to another avenue of learning from Jesus—being born from above.

✍ **Allow some time for members to encourage one another to read the Devotional and Scripture Readings and do the exercise in the following chapter before the next meeting.** Then invite the members to be silent for a few moments before leading them in reading the Closing Prayer aloud together.

CLOSING PRAYER

The Lord is my shepherd, I shall not want.
    He makes me lie down in green pastures;
he leads me beside still waters;
    he restores my soul.
He leads me in right paths
    for his name's sake.

Even though I walk through the darkest valley,
    I fear no evil;
for you are with me;
    your rod and your staff—
    they comfort me.

You prepare a table before me
    in the presence of my enemies;
you anoint my head with oil;
    my cup overflows.
Surely goodness and mercy shall follow me
    all the days of my life,
and I shall dwell in the house of the LORD
    my whole life long. (PS 23)

At the end of the Closing Prayer, the leader asks for a volunteer to lead the next meeting.

TAKING IT FURTHER

As a group or on your own, watch the movie *The Gospel of John* (Vision Bible International, 2003), which is a word-for-word narration of the fourth Gospel. See what insight this presentation gives you about the life of Jesus and Jesus's role in the Trinity.

ADDITIONAL EXERCISE

Saint Augustine. *Fifteen Books of Aurelius Augustinus, Bishop of Hippo, On the Trinity*. Translated by Philip Schaff. New York: Christian Literature Publishing, 1890.

Bettenson, Henry, ed. *Documents of the Christian Church*. New York: Oxford Univ. Press, 1963.

Charry, Ellen. "Spiritual Formation by the Doctrine of the Trinity." *Theology Today* (October 1997).

Foster, Richard J. *Streams of Living Water*. San Francisco: HarperSanFrancisco, 1998.

ADDITIONAL RESOURCES

What do you think your life would look like if the light of God wasn't present in it?

ADDITIONAL REFLECTION QUESTIONS

Should modern Christians spend more time struggling with difficult theological concepts, such as the Trinity, as did the members of the early church? Why or why not?

If someone asked you, how would you explain Jesus's relationship to God the Father? God the Holy Spirit?

3

EXPERIENCING THE SECOND BIRTH

KEY SCRIPTURE: John 3:1–15 and Luke 19:1–10

DEVOTIONAL READING

JOHN WESLEY, "The Marks of the New Birth"

"So is every man that is born of the Spirit." John [3:8].

How is every one that is "born of the Spirit,"—that is, born again,—born of God? What is meant by the being born again, the being born of God, or being born of the Spirit? . . . [W]hat is the new birth? . . . I propose to lay down the marks of it in the plainest manner, just as I find them laid down in Scripture.

I. 1. The first of these, and the foundation of all the rest, is faith. . . . The true, living Christian faith, which whosoever hath is born of God, is not only assent, an act of the understanding; but a disposition, which God hath wrought in his heart; "a sure trust and confidence in God, that through the merits of Christ his sins are forgiven, and he reconciled to the favour of God.". . .

II. 1. A second scriptural mark of those who are born of God, is hope. Thus St. Peter, . . . saith, "Blessed be the God and Father of our Lord Jesus Christ, which according to his abundant mercy, hath begotten us again unto a lively hope," 1 Peter [1:3]. . . . And thus is the Scripture fulfilled, "Blessed are they that mourn, for they shall be comforted." For it is easy to believe, that though sorrow may precede this witness of God's Spirit with our spirit; (indeed *must*, in some degree, while we groan under fear, and a sense of the wrath of God abiding on us;) yet, as soon as any man feeleth it in himself, his "sorrow is turned into joy." Whatsoever his pain may have been before; yet, as soon as that "hour is come, he remembereth the anguish no more, for joy" that he is born of God.

It is helpful for everyone to read the Devotional and Scripture Readings and do the My Life with God Exercise before the meeting. Begin the meeting with silent prayer, then move directly to Reflecting on My Life with God below.

III. 1. A third scriptural mark of those who are born of God, and the greatest of all, is love; even "the love of God shed abroad in their hearts, by the Holy Ghost which is given unto them," Rom. [5:5]. . . .

IV. 1. Thus I have plainly laid down those marks of the new birth which I find laid down in Scripture. Thus doth God himself answer that weighty question, what is it to be born of God? Such, if the appeal be made to the oracles of God, is "every one that is born of the Spirit." This it is, in the judgment of the Spirit of God, to be a son or a child of God. It is, so to *believe* in God, through Christ, as "not to commit sin," and to enjoy at all times, and in all places, that "peace of God which passeth all understanding." It is, so to *hope* in God through the Son of his love, as to have not only the "testimony of a good conscience," but also the spirit of God "bearing witness with your spirits, that ye are the children of God;" whence cannot but spring, the rejoicing evermore in him, through whom ye "have received the atonement." It is so to *love* God, who hath thus loved you, as you never did love any creature: so that ye are constrained to love all men as yourselves; with a love not only ever burning in your hearts, but flaming out in all your actions and conversation, and making your whole life one "labour of love," one continued obedience to those commands, "Be ye merciful, as God is merciful;" "Be ye holy, as I the Lord am holy;" "Be ye perfect, as your father which is in heaven is perfect."[1]

MY LIFE WITH GOD EXERCISE

John Wesley speaks about three spiritual results of being born from above: faith (or trust), hope, and love. In the last paragraph he lists the temporal (earthly) outcomes these spiritual qualities will have: our trust in God will lead us to live a pure life and have inner peace; our hope in God will produce in us a good conscience, inward knowledge that we have a personal relationship with God, and everlasting joy; our love of God will help us love our neighbors as ourselves and engage in a life of service.

As soon as you can, set aside at least half an hour and take an inventory of your spiritual life. You may want to do this early in the morning so that you can think about it during the rest of the day. Write down the three qualities of the spirit Wesley mentions—faith, hope, and love— and beside them write down some ways each quality has been expressed in your life. You might think of specific incidents, recurring events or interactions, or perhaps emotions you had or reasons for performing certain actions.

Additional qualities that result from being born from above are the fruit of the Spirit listed in Galatians 5:22: love, joy, peace, patience, kindness, generosity, faithfulness, gentleness, and self-control. Add these qualities to your list, and write down any evidence of them in your life. After you have finished with the list, look at it and see if there are any qualities of the spirit or fruit of the Spirit that have nothing written next to them. If there are, write down some ideas about what you think should be their results, then make plans to fill in those blanks over the next few days. For example, if you couldn't think of a way you had demonstrated peace, then challenge yourself to try to mediate a disagreement you are party to or hold your tongue when you are tempted to speak words of dissension. Intentionally working at what is difficult for us helps train our spirits to eventually do those things naturally.

In what ways did you find the qualities of spirit or fruit of the Spirit manifested in your life? Did you find any lacking in your life? If so, did that lack surprise you? What did you do to start filling in those gaps?

REFLECTING ON MY LIFE WITH GOD
Allow each member a few moments to answer this question.

▶ **SCRIPTURE READING:** JOHN 3:1–15; LUKE 19:1–10

Nicodemus, the Jewish Leader

Now there was a Pharisee named Nicodemus, a leader of the Jews. He came to Jesus by night and said to him, "Rabbi, we know that you are a teacher who has come from God; for no one can do these signs that you do apart from the presence of God." Jesus answered him, "Very truly, I tell you, no one can see the kingdom of God without being born from above." Nicodemus said to him, "How can anyone be born after having grown old? Can one enter a second time into the mother's womb and be born?" Jesus answered, "Very truly, I tell you, no one can enter the kingdom of God without being born of water and Spirit. What is born of the flesh is flesh, and what is born of the Spirit is spirit. Do not be astonished that I said to you, 'You must be born from above.' The wind blows where it chooses, and you hear the sound of it, but you do not know where it comes from or where it goes. So it is with everyone who is born of the Spirit." Nicodemus said to him, "How can these things be?" Jesus answered him, "Are you a teacher of Israel, and yet you do not understand these things?

↩ After everyone has had a chance to respond to the question, ask a member to read this passage from Scripture.

"Very truly, I tell you, we speak of what we know and testify to what we have seen; yet you do not receive our testimony. If I have told you about earthly things and you do not believe, how can you believe if I tell you about heavenly things? No one has ascended into heaven except the one who descended from heaven, the Son of Man. And just as Moses lifted up the serpent in the wilderness, so must the Son of Man be lifted up, that whoever believes in him may have eternal life."

Zacchaeus, the Tax Collector

[Jesus] entered Jericho and was passing through it. A man was there named Zacchaeus; he was a chief tax collector and was rich. He was trying to see who Jesus was, but on account of the crowd he could not, because he was short in stature. So he ran ahead and climbed a sycamore tree to see him, because he was going to pass that way. When Jesus came to the place, he looked up and said to him, "Zacchaeus, hurry and come down; for I must stay at your house today." So he hurried down and was happy to welcome him. All who saw it began to grumble and said, "He has gone to be the guest of one who is a sinner." Zacchaeus stood there and said to the Lord, "Look, half of my possessions, Lord, I will give to the poor; and if I have defrauded anyone of anything, I will pay back four times as much." Then Jesus said to him, "Today salvation has come to this house, because he too is a son of Abraham. For the Son of Man came to seek out and to save the lost."

REFLECTION QUESTION Allow each person a few moments to respond to this question.

Would you describe yourself as more like Nicodemus or Zacchaeus? Why?

↪ After a brief discussion, choose one person to read this section.

▶▶ GETTING THE PICTURE

Throughout Jesus's ministry we see him dealing with people as individuals. When we compare the number of individual encounters Jesus has with the number of times we see him address a crowd, it seems clear that Jesus prefers this type of one-on-one interaction. From the woman at the well to Mary and Martha, Jesus meets people and changes their lives, in the present and eternally. Two prime examples of this type of interaction and its amazing results are the stories of Nicodemus and Zacchaeus.

Although Nicodemus and Zacchaeus are Jews living in the same area, their lifestyles and social positions are worlds apart. Nicodemus belongs to the Pharisees, a prominent religious group of first-century Judaism. As a Pharisee, he teaches adherents of the Jewish faith the fine points of following the law. Further, John tells us that Nicodemus is a member of the council, probably the Sanhedrin, the religious ruling body headquartered in the environs of the Temple. This places Nicodemus among the members of the ruling class.

At the opposite end of the social spectrum is Zacchaeus. Luke tells us that he was a wealthy tax collector. The Roman Empire farmed out the task of collecting taxes to wealthy foreigners, who hired locals like Zacchaeus to do the leg work. These men, known as publicans, collected taxes on goods going to market and on certain goods in the markets. It was a common practice for tax collectors to charge more than was prescribed and pocket the excess. Many times the excess charges left farmers and merchants in debt to the tax collectors and moneylenders. So it comes as no surprise that collectors and lenders were highly despised. In addition, the religious establishment considered publicans unclean, because they regularly came in contact with Gentiles and with Jews who were ritually impure. Their business practices and unclean status placed them alongside and sometimes in the same category as sinners (Matt 9:11; 11:19; Luke 15:1–2).

Jesus uses these very different men to teach two essential lessons about what it means to be born into the kingdom of God. As he tells Nicodemus, people must be born from above (born again) in order to see the kingdom of God. This rebirth does not concern earthly things—following the law—but is a purely spiritual birth that leads to eternal life. However, as we learn from the story of Zacchaeus, this spiritual and eternal rebirth leads to changes in outlook and behavior in the earthly present, as our commitment to God allows the Holy Spirit to make changes in our actions and our lives. Zacchaeus immediately understands that following Jesus requires him to make things right, to give away his possessions and offer restitution to those he has defrauded. This life-changing process of sanctification that Zacchaeus and, later, Nicodemus are beginning is an ongoing journey for all of us who have undergone this second birth.

▶▶▶ GOING DEEPER

Despite the dissimilarities in Nicodemus's and Zacchaeus's occupations and social standing, the kingdom of God was available to both. They had

✑ Have another member read this section.

only to reach out for it. Both men felt something was missing in their lives and put themselves in a position to have that need met, at personal risk to themselves. Nicodemus ventured out into the dark to find Jesus, risking his vocation and social standing. Zacchaeus was so eager to see and hear the traveling rabbi that he threw caution and decorum to the wind and climbed a tree to better see Jesus. Their efforts were rewarded with a personal encounter with Jesus that transformed them.

Both Nicodemus and Zacchaeus took that initial step of belief to enter into the eternal kingdom of God. Although it took a while for Nicodemus, like many of us, to make the switch from the religious ruler who had all of the answers to being a disciple of Jesus, we learn later in the Gospel of John that he finally did. Zacchaeus, however, grasped the teachings of Jesus with his whole being seemingly instantaneously. He perceived the kingdom of God and walked into it with his whole heart. We can almost hear the excitement in Zacchaeus's voice as he tells Jesus what he is going to do.

Finally, we notice in these two accounts the inward changes to Nicodemus's and Zacchaeus's hearts, which result in behavior and actions consistent with participation in the kingdom of God. After his conversation with Jesus, Nicodemus tried to appeal to the conscience of the chief priests and the Pharisees after their plot to arrest Jesus failed, but his argument fell on deaf ears (John 7:51). After Jesus was crucified, Nicodemus helped Joseph of Arimathea prepare the body for burial (John 19:39–40). These actions put Nicodemus at odds with his fellow religious leaders, but he did them anyway. For Zacchaeus, gone were the days of overcharging farmers and merchants on their taxes. Now they were repaid four times the amount he had unjustly collected. Zacchaeus's actions probably made him the talk of Jericho, but by incorporating the teachings of Jesus into his life he gained more than he lost.

REFLECTION QUESTION
Allow each person a few moments to respond.

How would you characterize your entry into the kingdom of God—slowly and thoughtfully like Nicodemus, immediately and with great enthusiasm like Zacchaeus, or something else?

▶▶▶▶ POINTING TO GOD

✍ Choose one member to read this section.

Twentieth-century British journalist Malcolm Muggeridge grew up hearing about God, but he never found Jesus in the church of his childhood or in socialism, which was the primary belief system of his family. He moved to India as a young man and there met Mother Teresa, a then unknown Albanian nun who was ministering to the Indian people. He was fascinated by religious belief and saw a great story in the nun. His interviews with Mother Teresa and the resulting documentary, *Something Beautiful for God,* made her famous the world over. The two corresponded for years, and she wrote to Muggeridge many times that she prayed he would come to Christ. In one letter, now famous, she compared him to Nicodemus. "You are to me like Nicodemus," she wrote, "and I am sure the answer is the same—'unless you become like a little child.' I am sure you will understand beautifully everything if you would only 'become' a little child in God's hands. Your longing for God is so deep. . . . Christ is longing to be your Food. Surrounded with fullness of living food, you allow yourself to starve."[2]

And like Nicodemus, Muggeridge took a great deal of time before he acceded to Mother Teresa's urging and, along with his wife, converted to Roman Catholicism in 1982. His second birth was followed by a feeling of peace. He wrote, "Our entry into the Church is settled, which gives me, not so much exhilaration as a deep peace; to quote my own words: A sense of homecoming, of picking up the threads of a lost life, of responding to a bell that had long been ringing, of taking a place at a table that had long been vacant."[3] After taking that great step of being born into the kingdom of God, Muggeridge found his entire outlook changed. He spent the rest of his life writing books about Jesus.

In one of these books, *Jesus Rediscovered,* Muggeridge described himself as a displaced person on this earth:

> This sense of being a stranger, which first came to me at the very beginning of my life, I have never quite lost, however engulfed I might be, at particular times and in particular circumstances, in earthly pursuits—whether through cupidity, vanity, or sensuality, three chains that bind us, three goads that drive us, three iron gates that isolate us in the tiny, dark dungeon of our ego. For me there has always been—and I count it the greatest of all blessings—a window never finally blacked out, a light never finally extinguished. Days or weeks or months might pass. Would it never return—the lostness? I strain my ears to hear it, like distant music; my eyes to see it, a very bright light very far away. Has it gone forever? And then—ah! the relief. Like slipping away from a sleeping embrace, silently shutting a door behind

one, tiptoeing off in the gray light of dawn—a stranger again. The only ultimate disaster that can befall us, I have come to realize, is to feel ourselves to be at home here on earth. As long as we are aliens, we cannot forget our true homeland, which is that other kingdom You proclaimed.[4]

The phenomenon Muggeridge described affects all of us. We are displaced persons here on our earthly journey. When we become disciples of Jesus we experience a taste of what it is to finally find our place, but we can never be truly at home on this earth. We can only look to the future and know that one day we will be part of the kingdom of God in all its fullness. We will, finally, be at home.

▶▶▶▶ GOING FORWARD

✍ Have another person read this section.

Like Nicodemus, Zacchaeus, and Muggeridge, we are all displaced persons until we enter the kingdom of God, whether we realize it or not. It is in accepting the salvation offered through Christ's atonement on the cross and the accompanying process of sanctification that we find our heart's true home. This is our second birth, our birth from above. As we learned from Jesus's encounters with Nicodemus and Zacchaeus, this birth is both temporal and eternal. Our salvation in Jesus is reflected by changes in our present lives. Just as Nicodemus argued with the council over Jesus's fate and then prepared Jesus's body for burial, as Zacchaeus gave away his possessions and made restitution to those he had cheated, as Malcolm Muggeridge wrote books about the faith he had been searching for all his life, we all find the Holy Spirit having its way with our lives and our actions. Where once we were displaced, we are now at home and engaged in the work of the kingdom.

REFLECTION QUESTION
Again, allow each member a few moments to answer this question.

Describe a time when you felt like a displaced person. Was your feeling due to a physical change such as a move or a new job, or did it have a more spiritual foundation?

✍ After everyone has had a chance to respond, the leader reads this paragraph.

This concludes our look at the second birth Jesus described. In the next chapter we will turn our attention to another avenue of learning from Jesus—how Jesus redefined blessedness in the Beatitudes.

CLOSING PRAYER

The LORD is my shepherd, I shall not want.
    He makes me lie down in green pastures;
he leads me beside still waters;
    he restores my soul.
He leads me in right paths
    for his name's sake.

Even though I walk through the darkest valley,
    I fear no evil;
for you are with me;
    your rod and your staff—
    they comfort me.

You prepare a table before me
    in the presence of my enemies;
you anoint my head with oil;
    my cup overflows.
Surely goodness and mercy shall follow me
    all the days of my life,
and I shall dwell in the house of the LORD
    my whole life long. (PS 23)

✍ Allow some time for members to encourage one another to read the Devotional and Scripture Readings and do the exercise in the following chapter before the next meeting. Then invite the members to be silent for a few moments before leading them in reading the Closing Prayer aloud together.

✍ At the end of the Closing Prayer, the leader asks for a volunteer to lead the next meeting.

TAKING IT FURTHER

ADDITIONAL EXERCISE

Write in your journal about a time when you had a heartwarming experience of Jesus Christ. What were the circumstances? What actions did the experience lead you to?

ADDITIONAL RESOURCES

Muggeridge, Malcolm. *Conversion: The Spiritual Journey of a Twentieth-Century Pilgrim.* Eugene, OR: Wipf & Stock, 2005.

Muggeridge, Malcolm. *Jesus Rediscovered.* Garden City, New York: Doubleday-Galilee, 1969.

Muggeridge, Malcolm, *Something Beautiful for God.* San Francisco: HarperSanFrancisco, 1986.

Wesley, John. *Sermons on Several Occasions, Part 1.* Whitefish, MT: Kessinger Publishing, 2003.

What does it mean to be born from above? What kind of changes did being born from above cause in your life?

What steps did you take to meet Jesus Christ? What did you risk in your commitment to him?

Which part of the kingdom of God do you tend to emphasize—the kingdom work of the present or the life to come? Why?

4

REDEFINING BLESSEDNESS

KEY SCRIPTURE: Matthew 5:1–12

DEVOTIONAL READING

DALLAS WILLARD, *The Divine Conspiracy*

What we have come to call the Sermon on the Mount is a concise state-ment of Jesus' teachings on how to actually live in the reality of God's present kingdom available to us from the very space surrounding our bodies.... Jesus deals with the two major questions humanity always faces. First there is the question of which life is the good life.... What came to be called the Beatitudes were given by him to help clarify this matter.... The second question Jesus deals with in the sermon concerns who is truly a good person.... Who is it, according to Jesus, that has the good life?

The Beatitudes of Jesus drive home his answer to this question. They are among the literary and religious treasures of the human race. Along with the Ten Commandments, the Twenty-third Psalm, the Lord's Prayer, and a very few other passages from the Bible, they are acknowledged by almost everyone to be among the highest expressions of religious insight and moral inspiration. We can savor them, affirm them, meditate upon them, and engrave them on plaques to hang on our walls. But a major question remains: How are we to *live* in response to them?...

It will help us know what to do—and what not to do—with the Beatitudes if we can discover what Jesus himself was doing with them. That should be the key to understanding them, for after all they are his Beatitudes, not ours to make of them what we will. And since great teachers and leaders always have a coherent message that they develop in an orderly way, we should assume that his teaching in the Beatitudes is a clarification or development of his primary theme in this talk and in

> ✍ It is helpful for everyone to read the Devotional and Scripture Readings and do the My Life with God Exercise before the meeting. Begin the meeting with silent prayer, then move directly to Reflecting on My Life with God below.

his life: *the availability of the kingdom of the heavens.* How then, do they develop that theme? . . .

Having ministered to the needs of the people crowding around him, [Jesus] desired to teach them and moved to a higher position in the landscape—"up on a hill" (Matt. 5:1 BV)—where they could see and hear him well. But he does not, as is so often suggested, withdraw from the crowd to give an esoteric discourse of sublime irrelevance to the crying need of those pressing upon him. Rather, in the *midst* of this mass of raw humanity, and with them hanging on every word—note that it is they who respond at the end of the discourse—Jesus teaches his students or apprentices, along with all who hear, about the meaning of the availability of the heavens.

I believe he used the method of "show and tell" to make clear the extent to which the kingdom is "on hand" to us. There were directly before him those who *had just received* from the heavens through him. The context makes this clear. He could point out in the crowd now this individual, who was "blessed" because The Kingdom Among Us had just reached out and touched them with Jesus' heart and voice and hands. . . .

No one is actually being told that they are better off for being poor, for mourning, for being persecuted, and so on, or that the conditions listed are recommended ways to well-being before God or man. Nor are the Beatitudes indications of who will be on top "after the revolution." *They are explanations and illustrations, drawn from the immediate setting, of the present availability of the kingdom through personal relationship to Jesus.*[1]

MY LIFE WITH GOD EXERCISE

This excerpt is only a small fraction of a chapter in *The Divine Conspiracy* that Dallas Willard devotes to the Beatitudes in, as he calls it, the Sermon on the Hill. He also writes, "Misunderstandings of the 'blesseds' given by Jesus in Matthew 5 and Luke 6 have caused much pain and confusion down through the ages and continue to do so today. Strangely enough, his blesseds have not uniformly been a blessing. For many they have proved to be nothing less than pretty poison."[2] Some people have understood the Beatitudes as a description of the ideal follower of Christ and, knowing that they couldn't live up to them, have left the Christian life of faith. Others say they focus on specific rewards as compensation for present suffering, kind of a "suffer now, respite later." Still others have spiritual-ized them to the extent that they have no meaning for our lives today.

Let's take a closer look at the Beatitudes. First, please read the Beati-tudes in Matthew 5:1–12. Then draw a line down the middle of an 8½ x 11 sheet of paper. At the top left write, "Past and present thoughts about the Beatitudes." At the top right put, "New insights about the Beatitudes." To help you start filling in the left side, you might ask yourself several questions. If the Beatitudes are new to you or less familiar, ask yourself what your first impressions are of the verses. What stands out to you and what meaning could you take from these verses and apply to your own life? If you've heard or read other interpretations of these verses, write down those interpretations. Think about these questions: Did the interpretations focus on the past, present, or future? Were the Beatitudes emphasized as being intended for a group or for individuals? Was one Beatitude emphasized over another, or were they treated equally? Or were they seen as progressive (the later verses representing more desir-able qualities or more blessings)? Was a connection ever made between the Beatitudes and the kingdom of God? What feelings did you have re-garding these teachings? Write down your best recollection of the ways you have been taught to understand and interpret the Beatitudes. It may take a couple of days or longer to remember all the interpretations you've heard, so don't hurry. No doubt you will remember things a little at a time, not all at once.

After you've studied the Beatitudes or recalled your understanding of the Beatitudes in the past, read the excerpt from *The Divine Conspir-acy* several times, considering the sentence "*They are explanations and illustrations, drawn from the immediate setting, of the present availability of the kingdom through personal relationship to Jesus*" in conjunction with the Beatitudes. It might help to find a quiet place for this part of the exercise, because many times God's Word works best on a heart at rest. Try to empty your mind of any extraneous matters that might keep you from concentrating on the Beatitudes and what Jesus is teaching those gathered on the hill ... and you. It may also help to ask the Holy Spirit for wisdom as you try to look with fresh eyes at these familiar verses. If there is anything that God desires for you, it is to understand his Word so that it can work down into your innermost being: "If any of you is lacking in wisdom, ask God, who gives to all generously and ungrudg-ingly, and it will be given you" (James 1:5). At the end of this time, put on the right side of the piece of paper any new insights you have into the Beatitudes.

REFLECTING ON MY
LIFE WITH GOD
Allow each member a few
moments to answer this
question.

What past insights/teachings about the Beatitudes stood out to you as you were doing the above exercise? What new insights did you have?

➤ SCRIPTURE READING: MATTHEW 5:1–12

✍ After everyone has
had a chance to respond
to the question, ask a
member to read this pas-
sage from Scripture.

When Jesus saw the crowds, he went up the mountain; and after he sat down, his disciples came to him. Then he began to speak, and taught them, saying:

"Blessed are the poor in spirit, for theirs is the kingdom of heaven.
"Blessed are those who mourn, for they will be comforted.
"Blessed are the meek, for they will inherit the earth.
"Blessed are those who hunger and thirst for righteousness, for they will be filled.
"Blessed are the merciful, for they will receive mercy.
"Blessed are the pure in heart, for they will see God.
"Blessed are the peacemakers, for they will be called children of God.
"Blessed are those who are persecuted for righteousness' sake, for theirs is the kingdom of heaven.
"Blessed are you when people revile you and persecute you and utter all kinds of evil against you falsely on my account. Rejoice and be glad, for your reward is great in heaven, for in the same way they persecuted the prophets who were before you."

REFLECTION QUESTION
Allow each person a few
moments to respond to
this question.

How do you think you would react to these words if you were part of the crowd listening to Jesus?

➤➤ GETTING THE PICTURE

✍ After a brief discus-
sion, choose one person
to read this section.

Before we explore how Jesus redefines blessedness in the Beatitudes, it is helpful to understand how and why he teaches the way he does. Jesus teaches by using not abstract academic speech or flowery poetic language, but concrete examples taken from the context in which he finds himself. This is why the parable form—an earthy story with an everlasting meaning—is so prominent in his teachings. Jesus's parables employ characters familiar to his audience (a shepherd, a widow, a farmer) and objects everyone knows (a lost sheep, a lost coin, sown seed) to teach an eternal truth. But Jesus's teaching goes beyond the parable. He answers questions from people in the crowd (Luke 12), addresses concerns of his family (Matt 12:46–50), and uses everyday things, such as unleavened bread and wine, to convey spiritual truths (Matt 26:26–29). His examples are concrete and physical.

Jesus corrects many cultural ideas that are widely accepted. We have several examples where Jesus turns common wisdom upside down. In his interaction with the rich young ruler (Luke 18:18–25), Jesus goes against the prevailing cultural understanding and says that the man's wealth does not indicate that he has received favorable treatment from God. In the parable of the good Samaritan (Luke 10:25–37), the assumption is that religious leaders will act as good neighbors, and that a Samaritan will not go out of his way to help a fallen Jew, because Jews and Samaritans hate each other. The religious leaders fail the test, however, and the Samaritan not only helps the fallen man but proves to be an exceptionally good neighbor by showing the beaten man mercy. By holding a conversation with the woman at the well (John 4), Jesus corrects the common misperception that women are unworthy to be taught because they can't understand the deeper things of life.

Jesus imparts information in his teaching, but he also sets out to change the lives of those with whom he speaks. Today most education focuses on dispensing information to students. The goal of teachers in Jesus's day is to make a significant change in the lives of their pupils. Teaching has to impact the person's life for it to be deemed of any value. Hence, Jesus's conversation with the woman caught in adultery concludes with a message about the universality of sin and guidance for the future. "'Woman, where are they? Has no one condemned you?' She said, 'No one, sir.' And Jesus said, 'Neither do I condemn you. Go your way, and from now on do not sin again'" (John 8:10–11). The long-term effect of the teaching is to change the woman's life, not to give her facts unconnected to her daily existence.

▶▶▶ GOING DEEPER

Reading the Beatitudes while keeping in mind the three ways that Jesus taught—using concrete examples that his audience could relate to, correcting assumptions and accepted practices, and seeking to change

✍ Have another member read this section.

people's lives rather than merely relaying information—leads us to several spiritual formation principles.

Everyone is welcomed into the kingdom of God. As Willard explains, "[The Beatitudes] serve to clarify Jesus' fundamental message: the free availability of God's rule and righteousness to all of humanity through reliance upon Jesus himself, the person now loose in the world."[3] Most likely this crowd was like other crowds who attended Jesus's teaching: a hodgepodge of humankind, including women, men, and children; religious leaders and congregants; blue-collar and white-collar workers; sinners and saints; rich and poor; Jews, Samaritans, and Gentiles; bronze and white and all of the shades in-between. The nine categories Jesus named probably would have touched everyone there at some point in their lives. Who hasn't ever mourned? Who hasn't ever wanted to be closer to God? Who hasn't ever wanted to have a pure heart? Regardless of their place in society or present condition, all are welcome.

Further, if we understand the Beatitudes as extending an open invitation to the kingdom of God, then it follows that the Beatitudes are *not* "conditions that guarantee God's approval, salvation, or blessing."[4] We are not required to be spiritual giants to be admitted into the kingdom of heaven. We do not have to be uncomforted in our grief over lost opportunities or lost loved ones. We do not have to despair over our feelings of intimidation when confronted by difficult people and problem situations. Nothing—our spiritual, emotional, or mental state, or our background or vocation—disqualifies us from entering the good life of the kingdom.

As is so often the case in spiritual formation, the Beatitudes are the reverse of what we expect. Ben Witherington III and Darlene Hyatt write in *The Renovaré Spiritual Formation Bible,* "The Beatitudes give us a radical inversion of blessedness in God's order. Jesus takes those people ordinarily thought to be unblessed and unblessable and shows that there is something about life in the kingdom of God that makes them blessed."[5] The Beatitudes give concrete examples of those people who were considered unblessable in Jewish society because they had done something wrong, or their relative had done something wrong, or they were born in the wrong place, or they had the wrong occupation, *ad infinitum.* So who is considered unblessable in our society? The fat, old, poor, illiterate, impotent, sick, immodest, disabled, immoral, thieves, *ad infinitum.* Things haven't changed much, have they? In the kingdom of heaven all are welcome, and we can be blessed in spite of everything.

The Beatitudes themselves and the invitation Jesus extends to enter the kingdom of God are timeless. This invitation is not only for certain

LEARNING FROM JESUS

people in a particular time, either past, present, or future. It is as applicable today as it was for the people who listened in person to Jesus on the mountain, and rightly understood, it will continue to be a source of help and encouragement to disciples of Jesus Christ as they take the good news of the kingdom throughout the world. All of us face the same issues Jesus addressed in the first-century Beatitudes—feelings of spiritual poverty, the desire to live a holy life, attempts to bring reconciliation, experiences of persecution—as will people throughout our century and the next one. Jesus's timeless invitation addresses those needs as it echoes through the corridors of the centuries and beyond: "Come to me, all you that are weary and are carrying heavy burdens, and I will give you rest" (Matt 11:28).

How do the words of Jesus in the Beatitudes speak to you in your present situation?

REFLECTION QUESTION
Allow each person a few moments to respond.

▶▶▶ POINTING TO GOD

✍ Choose one member to read this section.

Many Christian converts throughout history have testified to the availability of God's kingdom to all people. One example is John Newton, the British sailor and slave trader turned priest and hymn-writer. As a young man, Newton was known as the Great Blasphemer, famous among fellow sailors for his foul language and coarseness of manner. He even led other sailors into unbelief. But that all changed after one particularly awful storm at sea. On March 21, 1748, his ship was suffering through the eleventh day of a fierce North Atlantic storm. Newton had been lashed to the helm to try to control the ship's course. In a state of exhausted desperation, his mind turned to the verses his mother had taught him as a child, Proverbs 1:24–31: "Because I have called and you refused . . . I also will laugh at your calamity; I will mock when panic strikes you, when panic strikes you like a storm, and your calamity comes like a whirlwind, when distress and anguish come upon you. Then they will call upon me, but I will not answer." Newton despaired at this verse, but later he found a New Testament and started to read, stopping when he came to Luke 11:13: "If you then, who are evil, know how to give good gifts to your children, how much more will the heavenly Father give the Holy Spirit to those who ask him!"

Newton realized in that moment that God's kingdom was available even to him, rough and sinful as he was. He eventually left the sea and the slave-trading business behind and became a minister. During his forty-three-year ministry, he habitually composed hymns for the Sunday evening service. His most famous hymn, "Amazing Grace," marvels at the openness of God's kingdom to all people—wretches and sinners though we are. We can see a reflection of Newton's personal story in the first three verses:

> Amazing Grace! how sweet the sound,
> That saved a wretch like me!
> I once was lost, but now am found;
> Was blind, but now I see.
>
> 'Twas grace that taught my heart to fear,
> And grace my fears relieved;
> How precious did that grace appear
> The hour I first believed!
>
> Thro' many dangers, toils and snares,
> I have already come;
> 'Tis grace hath bro't me safe this far,
> And grace will lead me home.[6]

▶▶▶▶▶ GOING FORWARD

Have another person read this section.

Many of us are waiting for that indefinable moment when we'll get it all together. But Jesus is interested in our current circumstances and situations, where we are right now. It can be hard to accept that even the weakest person can be a working part of the kingdom of God. But we have to think that Jesus does not want us to wait around to reach some imaginary standard of worthiness. We will never deserve Jesus's atoning sacrifice. But it is offered to all of us just the same. Right now, as rough and rude and unpolished and sinful as we are, Jesus Christ will take us. And not just us, but those around us, even the ones we find off-putting and undeserving.

REFLECTION QUESTION
Again, allow each member a few moments to answer this question.

Have you ever felt unworthy of God's love? How did you deal with this feeling?

After everyone has had a chance to respond, the leader reads this paragraph.

This concludes our look at redefining blessedness. In the next chapter we will turn our attention to another avenue of learning from Jesus—his teachings about the Sabbath.

CLOSING PRAYER

The LORD is my shepherd, I shall not want.
    He makes me lie down in green pastures;
he leads me beside still waters;
    he restores my soul.
He leads me in right paths
    for his name's sake.

Even though I walk through the darkest valley,
    I fear no evil;
for you are with me;
    your rod and your staff—
    they comfort me.

You prepare a table before me
    in the presence of my enemies;
you anoint my head with oil;
    my cup overflows.
Surely goodness and mercy shall follow me
    all the days of my life,
and I shall dwell in the house of the LORD
    my whole life long. (PS 23)

Allow some time for members to encourage one another to read the Devotional and Scripture Readings and do the exercise in the following chapter before the next meeting. Then invite the members to be silent for a few moments before leading them in reading the Closing Prayer aloud together.

At the end of the Closing Prayer, the leader asks for a volunteer to lead the next meeting.

TAKING IT FURTHER

ADDITIONAL EXERCISES

- Come up with your own version of the Beatitudes, tailored to those people you see around you who may be considered unblessable by the rules of society. Why do you think these people are not considered by others to be prime candidates for the kingdom of God?

- Memorize Matthew 5:1–12.

ADDITIONAL RESOURCES

Bonhoeffer, Dietrich. *The Cost of Discipleship.* New York: Simon & Schuster/Touchstone, 1995.
Willard, Dallas. *The Divine Conspiracy.* San Francisco: HarperSanFrancisco, 1998.

What would you say to someone who told you he or she was unworthy of the kingdom of God?

Jesus shocked many people with his assertion that all were welcome in the kingdom of God. If we are honest with ourselves, most of us can think of some individuals or groups of people that we don't expect to be in the kingdom of God. Who do you tend not to see as blessed?

What pieces of common wisdom might Jesus need to correct in today's world?

5 FREEING THE SABBATH

DEVOTIONAL READING

VIRGINIA STEM OWENS, *Looking for Jesus*

My generation will probably be the last that remembers "blue laws," those now antique attempts to impose Sabbath sanctity on the operation of businesses. Up till the 1960s, practically all stores, at least in my part of the country, were required by law to close on Sundays. Department stores, supermarkets, most service stations, in some places even movie theaters, shut down on that day. At most, a few restaurants in town stayed open in order to accommodate the after-church diners—although some congregations refrained from patronizing such establishments on Sunday, sometimes all week.

But life in general proceeded at a more peaceful pace then. Not only did our town observe the fourth commandment, to "remember the sabbath day, to keep it holy," it didn't have interstate highways punctuated with McDonald's, which would later encourage weekend trips and non-stop Sunday sports marathons. Particularly devout families sometimes had their own peculiar rules about what was and was not acceptable Sabbath behavior. In mine, for instance, no one was allowed to read the comics from the newspaper until after church. This will strike many as quaint or even silly today, but such customs were a way of following the commandment's injunction to "remember."

You never forgot it was Sunday when I was a child. You wore special clothes on that day—your "Sunday best," including your best underwear—and ate special food, usually pot roast or fried chicken. The day made a small blip of celebration in my parents' otherwise flat-line workweek. My father was glad to put aside his paintbrush and ladder, and my mother was grateful the Bible freed her from the wringer washer and

✍ It is helpful for everyone to read the Devotional and Scripture Readings and do the My Life with God Exercise before the meeting. Begin the meeting with silent prayer, then move directly to Reflecting on My Life with God below.

clothesline at least one day a week. They were both thankful for their own rest and sympathetic with a like need in waitresses and delivery boys....

As likely as not, we see Sunday as a chance for exercise, a time for physical exertion at a health club or ball game to make sure our muscles don't atrophy.... And those averse to exercise want entertainment, not reflection, distraction rather than rest. These days, we want *more* to do on Sundays, not less. For us the Sabbath means forgetting, not remembering.

No single subject was disputed more often between Jesus and the Pharisees than the kinds of activity permissible on the Sabbath. This was not a novel issue for debate then. The boundaries of Sabbath-keeping had been disputed for generations. The Pharisees and Sadducees had argued about whether the golden table in the Temple, where the twelve shewbread loaves were displayed, should be washed on the Sabbath.... For Jews of the first century, Sabbath keeping (along with the physical, though not visible, sign of circumcision) provided the outward sign that set them apart from the surrounding pagans.[1]

MY LIFE WITH GOD EXERCISE

Before we discuss the Devotional Reading, let's look more closely at the historical background of the Sabbath. In the Ten Commandments, God commanded the people to rest on the seventh day of the week (Exod 20:8–11), the day on which the Lord rested after creating the heavens and the earth (Gen 2:2–3). As in the creation story, this period was generally understood to last from evening to evening. A glance at most calendars or dictionaries will confirm that the seventh day of the week is Saturday. Along with other Jews of his time, Jesus and the rest of the disciples celebrated the Sabbath on the seventh day (although Jesus's interpretation of honoring the Sabbath differed from that of some religious authorities of the time, as we will see in the Scripture Reading below).

But after Jesus's death and resurrection, early Christians started to meet and break bread together on Sunday, the first day of the week (Acts 20:7). Although many followers who came from the Jewish tradition continued to honor the Saturday Sabbath as well, the meetings on Sunday, the first day of the week, stuck. Sunday became known as the "Lord's day" (Rev 1:10). It's unclear what started this tradition. Some say that early Christians met on the first day rather than the seventh to avoid persecution; others point out that Jesus's resurrection occurred on the first day of the week, the day after the Sabbath, so it is appropriate for

Christians to meet on that day. Whatever the reason, many Christians throughout history and today not only attend church on Sundays but also treat Sunday as the Sabbath, a day of rest to be observed and honored in much the same way as Jews honor the Sabbath.

We find this mindset in the Devotional Reading, when Virginia Stem Owens describes how her family observed the Christian Sabbath, or Lord's day, when she was growing up. She also recalls her parents' relief and thankfulness as they relaxed and rested from their labors. This week examine your own feelings regarding the Sabbath or the Lord's day. You might begin by considering whether you see a distinction between the two terms. It might be helpful to write down both terms and make a list of your reactions to each. Try to be honest with yourself. If you consider *Sabbath* and *Lord's day* to be synonymous, consider why. If you feel they are different, describe how they have been different in your life. Feel free to write down positive and negative connotations for each term. Next, think about how your family did or did not practice a Christian Sabbath or Lord's day. Does your experience resemble that of Virginia Stem Owens? Did you have your own peculiar rules or traditions? Or did your family treat Saturday or Sunday just like any other day? Consider how your opinion or practice has changed during the stages of your life: childhood, youth, young adult, and adult.

Next, think more about what is meant by "a day of rest." You could even consult a concordance and look up the verses that mention rest—for example, Mark 6:31 and Matthew 11:28. What would a day of rest look like for you? What would and wouldn't it entail? On the weekend, commit yourself to putting these ideas into action with a real day of rest. If this is already your practice on Saturday or Sunday, then try to be especially mindful about your day of rest this week and its effect on you and those around you.

How did your day of rest go? What new insights did you have about the Sabbath or the Lord's day and its place in your life?

REFLECTING ON MY LIFE WITH GOD
Allow each member a few moments to answer this question.

➤ SCRIPTURE READING: MARK 2:23–3:6

One sabbath [Jesus] was going through the grainfields; and as they made their way his disciples began to pluck heads of grain. The Pharisees said to him, "Look, why are they doing what is not lawful on the sabbath?" And he said to them, "Have you never read what David did when he and

After everyone has had a chance to respond to the question, ask a member to read this passage from Scripture.

his companions were hungry and in need of food? He entered the house of God, when Abiathar was high priest, and ate the bread of the Presence, which it is not lawful for any but the priests to eat, and he gave some to his companions." Then he said to them, "The sabbath was made for humankind, and not humankind for the sabbath; so the Son of Man is lord even of the sabbath."

Again he entered the synagogue, and a man was there who had a withered hand. They watched him to see whether he would cure him on the sabbath, so that they might accuse him. And he said to the man who had the withered hand, "Come forward." Then he said to them, "Is it lawful to do good or to do harm on the sabbath, to save life or to kill?" But they were silent. He looked around at them with anger; he was grieved at their hardness of heart and said to the man, "Stretch out your hand." He stretched it out, and his hand was restored. The Pharisees went out and immediately conspired with the Herodians against him, how to destroy him.

REFLECTION QUESTION
Allow each person a few moments to respond to this question.

How do you interpret the statement, "The sabbath was made for humankind, and not humankind for the sabbath"?

▶▶ GETTING THE PICTURE

◁⧸ After a brief discussion, choose one person to read this section.

In the first paragraph, the Pharisees question whether the actions of Jesus and his disciples are lawful on the Sabbath. In the second, they watch Jesus, and when they again find his behavior inappropriate and unlawful for the Sabbath, they conspire with the Herodians to "destroy" him. Before looking more closely at what Jesus is saying in this passage, let's set the context by learning more about the Pharisees. Not only in this passage but many times in the Gospels, "the Pharisees" are cast in the role of antagonists. It seems that Jesus couldn't say or do anything to please them. At first glance, Jesus appears to confront the teachings of the whole group (for examples see Matt 15:1–9; Luke 14:1–6; John 5:2–18; 7:10–23), but further study shows this is not the case. There were two schools of Pharisees during the first century: Hillels and Shammais. Today we would categorize the Hillels as theological moderates and the Shammais as theological legalists. Jesus's disagreements would have been mostly with the Shammai Pharisees.

The Shammai school tended toward fundamental interpretations of and strict adherence to the Mosaic law and oral tradition. Moderate

LEARNING FROM JESUS

rabbis and scholars had made exceptions to the Sabbath law for special events, such as cooking for an ill person, saving someone's life, alleviating pain, and attending to a snake bite. Certain rabbis also condoned acts of service on the Sabbath. The two schools, Hillel and Shammai, publicly debated the limits of the concessions to be made in order to correctly observe the Sabbath, so Jesus was not the only one to challenge the strict interpretations of the Shammai school. What was unusual was not that Jesus confronted the rigidity of the Shammai school of Pharisees, but that their reaction to him was so strong. It makes us wonder if they felt Jesus was trying to usurp their authority and power rather than just confront their legalistic mindset.

Contrary to what many Christians have been taught, the Pharisees were well respected by first-century Jews. Even though they had their own internal rules, the Pharisees knew the Mosaic law and the oral traditions well. Rabbi Hillel, the founder of the moderate school of Pharisees, was especially adept at halachic (legal) interpretation, a never-ending attempt to reconcile discrepancies within the Mosaic law. In their service in local synagogues, the Pharisees who served as rabbis devoted much effort to enforcing the regulations for sacrifices, ritual purity, dues to the temple, tithing, observance of the Sabbath and other festivals, vows, marriages, and issues faced in everyday religious life. Following God and encouraging the people to follow God in the same way was important to the Pharisees, and to have Jesus attract so many followers while actively disregarding their teachings could easily have put their authority in jeopardy.

▶▶▶ GOING DEEPER

When pondering the meaning of the Scripture Reading for our lives today, many times we find ourselves pointing fingers at the Pharisees and saying to ourselves, "What hypocrites. They were so intent on following the law to the letter that they violated the admonition to 'love your neighbor as yourself'" (Lev 19:18b; Matt 19:19b). It takes much pondering, prayer, and time to overcome the propensity to find fault in others before we see it in ourselves, but it is a worthy goal. The ability to see our own faults sharpens as we become more fully formed in the image of Christ. Pulling spiritual formation principles from Scripture helps us continue on that path.

In the Scripture Reading we find the principle that we should always pay attention to human need, particularly the need of others. The

Have another member read this section.

people around us are more important than our schedules and, often, more important than our other priorities. This is not to say that their needs should always come first, but there are times when responding to human need must be our top priority. For example, it might be better to end your prayer time early to answer a phone call from a troubled friend or miss a church service to visit a sick family member.

How comforting it would be to know that for every situation we could possibly encounter, there is a law or rule that tells us just what to do. Unfortunately, it doesn't work that way. Laws are not meant to turn us into robots. Jesus taught that regulations are supposed to enhance human life, not reduce it to a formula. For this reason, the Mosaic law had exceptions and safeguards built into it. For example, if a family couldn't present its yearly tithe to the Lord in Jerusalem, they were supposed to sell the animals and produce and use the money to throw a party (Deut 14:22–27). These holes in the law provided for human needs and special situations. The mistake the Shammai Pharisees made was trying to fill those holes while ignoring human needs. With the best intentions of honoring God, the legalists of Jesus's time nonetheless made the mistake of trying to shoehorn humans into their idea of what a good life should look like. They had forgotten that the ideal good life cannot be thoroughly mapped.

Jesus helped us understand the reaction of the Pharisees by explaining that they suffered from hardness of heart. We should grieve over this hardness of heart—not only our own but that of those we love and work with and those with whom we come into casual contact. Hardness of heart does not necessarily entail a lack of belief in God, although that is one kind of hardness. The hardness of heart from which the Pharisees suffered comes from studying the Scriptures and believing in God for some time. There are dangers inherent in each step of the Christian life, and a particular danger at this point is jadedness toward the things of God. Like the old saying "Familiarity breeds contempt," we think we know all the answers and lose our sense of wonder and awe and thankfulness and humility. It is an ever-present danger that should be the subject of our humble prayers.

There is a point in the spiritual life when it is okay to challenge authority, even to get angry. In our Scripture Reading we see that Jesus became angry when the Pharisees didn't answer his question about whether it was permissible to do good on the Sabbath. It is clear that he was angry not because they were ignoring him but because the Pharisees were silent at the expense of a man's welfare. Jesus did not express his anger in the ways we might expect. His anger led him to *grieve* for the Pharisees. Jesus did not yell at the Pharisees or stomp out of the synagogue. Instead he focused on the human need of the man in the synagogue and healed his withered hand. Jesus made a very public statement about what is appropriate on the Sabbath. He put the man's need first and, at the same time, corrected an injustice. We should always exercise extreme caution when we find anger in ourselves. But when our anger concerns the welfare of others, it can be appropriate, because many times that anger will motivate us to correct the injustice.

We can learn a great deal from Jesus's statement, "The sabbath was made for humankind, and not humankind for the sabbath." This is a reminder of both the value and the limitations of the rules that govern a Christian life. The rules that God sets out for us in the Bible and in our ongoing relationship with him are not arbitrary; they show that God knows better than we what will satisfy us and ultimately make us happy. For example, the Sabbath day of rest is not intended for penitence but as a God-designed way for us to refresh ourselves and enjoy our families and God. With this purpose in mind, we should be careful about promoting standards and practices that turn our Sabbath into a day filled with dos and don'ts. In Galatians, the apostle Paul writes, "For freedom Christ has set us free" (5:1a). God instituted a day of rest, the Jewish Sabbath, so that humans could rest from their labors, not for them to worry about what regulations or laws they might break, or to place that rest above the welfare and needs of those around them. The Christian Sabbath, the Lord's day, is a time for us to assemble with other believers and remember all that the Lord has done for us and promises to do for us in the future.

In what areas of the Christian life do you find yourself leaning toward legalism?

REFLECTION QUESTION
Allow each person a few moments to respond.

▶▶▶▶ POINTING TO GOD

Just as Jesus challenged the legalism of the Pharisees over the Sabbath, throughout Christian history people have challenged the religious authorities over practices they felt did not honor the foundational principles of Christianity. Certainly one of the most notable of these is Martin Luther, the sixteenth-century German ecclesiastical reformer who famously nailed his ninety-five theses to the door of the Castle Church

✍ Choose one member to read this section.

at Wittenberg. Luther's main quarrel with the leadership of the Catholic Church was over the selling of indulgences. At that time, parishioners could purchase, for themselves or for deceased relatives, an indulgence that would gain them early release from purgatory. The money from the indulgences went into the church coffers. Luther's concern was that the sale of indulgences was leading Christians away from the process of confession and repentance. He was branded a heretic by Pope Leo X, but this controversy was only the beginning of Luther's quarrels with the religious authorities of his time. He disagreed with the pope over papal authority, the administering of the sacraments, clerical celibacy, and other issues large and small, and was eventually excommunicated. Luther is now credited with helping shape the Protestant Reformation. Looking back, we see in him an example of the righteous anger Jesus demonstrated; Luther further possessed, like Jesus, the courage to challenge authority and a commitment to correct injustice.

Also like Jesus, Luther never challenged the authority of the law as revealed by the Bible, just additional rules and regulations created by religious authorities who had tried to fill in blanks and exceptions to the law. Luther believed that the law had to be internalized, not imposed externally in this way. He wrote, "In [Romans] 7, St. Paul says, 'The law is spiritual.' What does that mean? If the law were physical, then it could be satisfied by works, but since it is spiritual, no one can satisfy it unless everything he does springs from the depths of the heart. But no one can give such a heart except the Spirit of God, who makes the person be like the law, so that he actually conceives a heartfelt longing for the law and henceforward does everything, not through fear or coercion, but from a free heart."[2]

Rather than focusing on the orderly functioning of the Church and the promotion of its interests, Luther focused on loving God and loving neighbor. He perceived that many activities the clergy encouraged did not help the faithful develop a spiritual mind or a heart capable of unconditional love. For this reason, he moved away from the legalisms of his time. In his own way, Luther was freeing the Sabbath.

➤➤➤➤➤ GOING FORWARD

Have another person read this section.

The Sabbath has been a source of disagreement for Jews since before the time of Jesus. Indeed, much of the "law" that we find in the Old

LEARNING FROM JESUS

and New Testaments has been and is still debated inside the Church. However we celebrate the Sabbath and keep the commands we find in Scripture, these matters come into focus when we look at them through the lens of Jesus's statement that the Sabbath is made for humankind and not vice versa. Jesus teaches us that we must always prioritize the needs of those around us over external rules and regulations. As Jesus said, he did not come to abolish the law, but to fulfill it (Matt 5:17); Jesus's freedom came not through keeping the letter of the law, but by developing the spirit of the law within himself. As we become ever more Christlike, we will find that the law is written on our hearts, guiding us from within and calling us to love God and one another. Another quotation from Martin Luther is most appropriate: "What is it to serve God and do His will? Nothing else than to show mercy to our neighbor. For it is our neighbor who needs our service; God in heaven needs it not."

What does it mean to you to internalize the law?

REFLECTION QUESTION
Again, allow each member a few moments to answer this question.

This concludes our look at freeing the Sabbath. In the next chapter we will turn our attention to another avenue of learning from Jesus—feasting on the Word.

⤳ After everyone has had a chance to respond, the leader reads this paragraph.

⤳ **Allow some time for members to encourage one another to read the Devotional and Scripture Readings and do the exercise in the following chapter before the next meeting.** Then invite the members to be silent for a few moments before leading them in reading the Closing Prayer aloud together.

CLOSING PRAYER

The LORD is my shepherd, I shall not want.
    He makes me lie down in green pastures;
he leads me beside still waters;
    he restores my soul.
He leads me in right paths
    for his name's sake.

Even though I walk through the darkest valley,
    I fear no evil;
for you are with me;
    your rod and your staff—
    they comfort me.

You prepare a table before me
    in the presence of my enemies;
you anoint my head with oil;
    my cup overflows.

Surely goodness and mercy shall follow me
all the days of my life,
and I shall dwell in the house of the LORD
my whole life long. (PS 23)

TAKING IT FURTHER

ADDITIONAL EXERCISE

If your congregation meets on Sunday, attend a service on Saturday at a Roman Catholic, Episcopal, or Seventh-Day Adventist church. If your church meets on Saturday, try attending a service on Sunday. What does it feel like to worship on the seventh day if you are used to the first day, or vice versa?

ADDITIONAL RESOURCES

Bainton, Roland. *Here I Stand: A Life of Martin Luther*. Nashville, TN: Abingdon, 1990.
Marty, Martin. *Martin Luther: A Penguin Life*. New York: Penguin, 2004.
Owens, Virginia Stem. *Looking for Jesus*. Louisville, KY: Westminster/ John Knox, 1998.

ADDITIONAL REFLECTION QUESTIONS

What, if any, is the difference between Virginia Stem Owens's family rule about not reading the comics until after church and the kind of legalism Jesus spoke against?

How would you react if your pastor told you that taking communion or visiting a sick person on Sunday would violate church rules?

Has hardness of heart been a problem in your life? If so, in what way—jadedness with God or another manifestation of hardness of heart?

FEASTING ON THE WORD

6

DEVOTIONAL READING

FREDERICK BUECHNER, *The Hungering Dark*

The world is full of people who seem to have listened to the wrong voice and are now engaged in life-work in which they find no pleasure or purpose and who run the risk of suddenly realizing someday that they have spent the only years that they are ever going to get in this world doing something which could not matter less to themselves or to anyone else. This does not mean, of course, people who are doing work that from the outside looks unglamourous and humdrum, because obviously such work as that may be a crucial form of service and deeply creative. But it means people who are doing work that seems simply irrelevant not only to the great human needs and issues of our time but also to their own need to grow and develop as humans.

In John Marquand's novel *Point of No Return,* for instance, after years of apple-polishing and bucking for promotion and dedicating all his energies to a single goal, Charlie Gray finally gets to be vice-president of the fancy little New York bank where he works; and then the terrible moment comes when he realizes that it is really not what he wanted after all, when the prize that he has spent his life trying to win suddenly turns to ashes in his hands. His promotion assures him and his family of all the security and standing that he has always sought, but Marquand leaves you with the feeling that maybe the best way Charlie Gray could have supported his family would have been by giving his life to the kind of work where he could have expressed himself and fulfilled himself in such a way as to become in himself, as a person, the kind of support they really needed.

> ⬂ It is helpful for everyone to read the Devotional and Scripture Readings and do the My Life with God Exercise before the meeting. Begin the meeting with silent prayer, then move directly to Reflecting on My Life with God below.

There is also the moment in the Gospels where Jesus is portrayed as going into the wilderness for forty days and nights and being tempted there by the devil. And one of the ways that the devil tempts him is to wait until Jesus is very hungry from fasting and then to suggest that he simply turn the stones into bread and eat. Jesus answers, "Man shall not live by bread alone," and this just happens to be, among other things, true, and very close to the same truth that Charlie Gray comes to when he realizes too late that he was not made to live on status and salary alone but that something crucially important was missing from his life even though he was not sure what it was any more than, perhaps, Marquand himself was sure what it was.

There is nothing moralistic or sentimental about this truth. It means for us simply that we must be careful with our lives, for Christ's sake, because it would seem that they are the only lives we are going to have in this puzzling and perilous world, and so they are very precious and what we do with them matters enormously. Everybody knows that. We need no one to tell it to us. . . .

Jesus said, "Man shall not live by bread alone, but by every word that proceeds from the mouth of God," and in the end every word that proceeds from the mouth of God is the same word, and the word is Christ himself. And in the end that is the vocation, the calling of all of us, the calling to be Christs. To be Christs in whatever way we are able to be. To be Christs with whatever gladness we have and in whatever place, among whatever brothers we are called to. That is the vocation, the destiny to which we were all of us called even before the foundations of the world.[1]

MY LIFE WITH GOD EXERCISE

Buechner uses the example of Charlie Gray to explain that God did not create us to focus only on temporal, physical rewards, such as social status and money in the bank. He then quotes Jesus's admonition that we need something beyond the food that satisfies our physical bellies—that God has made us with a spiritual dimension that needs nurturing. What we do, in terms of our everyday actions and our lifelong vocation, is important because it has spiritual and eternal implications. We need to keep both the daily and the eternal in mind, harmonizing the spiritual with the physical. To enable that process, we feed on the Word and become "little Christs," the literal meaning of the Greek word that is translated as "Christian" (see Acts 11:26). In John 6:25–40 Jesus again emphasizes this point as he tells the crowd that they should shift their focus from physical food to spiritual food. Jesus specifies that the source of the spiritual food is God the Father, and that he has come down from heaven to bring that food to them.

These are difficult concepts for most of us. We are so attuned to the physical aspects of life that it is hard to turn our focus 180 degrees to the spiritual or unseen dimension of our existence. In this chapter's exercise we ask you to consider the way the physical and the spiritual work together in your life. Start by going for a walk and focusing on the physical. Touch things. Deliberately listen to the sounds of nature and humans. Concentrate on noticing colors. Smell the air. Listen to your body. Are you hungry? Does a muscle ache here and there? Are you cold? Hot?

Next, try to shift your attention to the nonphysical by fasting for at least one meal. (If you have a medical condition that makes it inadvisable for you to skip meals, skip a favorite television show or another activity you enjoy.) Use what would have been your mealtime to study the Bible and pray. Try to focus on the spiritual side of your life for the entire time you are fasting. Concentrate on your emotions when talking with colleagues or family, your reactions to reading the Bible and praying, your thoughts as you watch an athletic event or pay your bills. Are they negative or positive? Do they draw you closer to God or drive a wedge between yourself and God? Consider your vocation or planned vocation. Are you operating under the assumption that what you do matters? Is your choice or practice of a vocation driven by an eternal view of life or is it more closely aligned with physical needs and wants?

Finally, as you near the end of your fast, try to think about both the physical and nonphysical aspects of your life. Take another walk. This time consider your reactions to the things you see, hear, and touch. Think about how your reactions to the things around you and your own body make you feel. Consider your fasting experience: has choosing to deny your body's hunger or desires for a period of time helped you to focus more on spiritual things? Or did your mind dwell even more on your physical cravings? What insights did fasting give you as to how your body and spirit work together, fuel each other?

To break your fast from food, eat a small meal very slowly and intentionally. Pay attention to each bite, considering the role and purpose of food in your life. Thank God for the nourishment the food gives to your body. Finally, take some time to consider what it means that Jesus called himself the bread of life.

If you like to write, you can jot down your observations about the physical and the nonphysical, but don't feel obligated to put anything in writing. Or you might find it more helpful to discuss with a close friend what you have discovered about yourself. Sometimes we spontaneously say things that give us insight into our lives.

REFLECTING ON MY LIFE WITH GOD
Allow each member a few moments to answer this question.

What did you find out about yourself as you were doing the exercise? Were you more attuned to the physical than the spiritual or vice versa? Can you think of ways to bring the physical and spiritual into balance?

➤ SCRIPTURE READING: JOHN 6:25–40

After everyone has had a chance to respond to the question, ask a member to read this passage from Scripture.

When [the crowd] found him on the other side of the sea, they said to him, "Rabbi, when did you come here?" Jesus answered them, "Very truly, I tell you, you are looking for me, not because you saw signs, but because you ate your fill of the loaves. Do not work for the food that perishes, but for the food that endures for eternal life, which the Son of Man will give you. For it is on him that God the Father has set his seal." Then they said to him, "What must we do to perform the works of God?" Jesus answered them, "This is the work of God, that you believe in him whom he has sent." So they said to him, "What sign are you going to give us then, so that we may see it and believe you? What work are you performing? Our ancestors ate the manna in the wilderness; as it is written, 'He gave them bread from heaven to eat.'" Then Jesus said to them, "Very truly, I tell you, it was not Moses who gave you the bread from heaven, but it is my Father who gives you the true bread from heaven. For the bread of God is that which comes down from heaven and gives life to the world." They said to him, "Sir, give us this bread always."

Jesus said to them, "I am the bread of life. Whoever comes to me will never be hungry, and whoever believes in me will never be thirsty. But I said to you that you have seen me and yet do not believe. Everything that the Father gives me will come to me, and anyone who comes to me I will never drive away; for I have come down from heaven, not to do my own will, but the will of him who sent me. And this is the will of him who sent me, that I should lose nothing of all that he has given me, but raise it up on the last day. This is indeed the will of my Father, that all who see the Son and believe in him may have eternal life; and I will raise them up on the last day."

If you had been in the crowd that had eaten its fill of the loaves and then was told by Jesus that he was the bread of life, how do you think you would have felt?

REFLECTION QUESTION
Allow each person a few moments to respond to this question.

▶▶ GETTING THE PICTURE

The Scripture Reading from the Gospel of John continues an account of the previous day, when Jesus performed a miracle by multiplying five barley loaves and two fish into enough food to satisfy the physical appetites of thousands of people. When the crowd realized what had happened, they decided to make Jesus king by force, so he left them and "withdrew again to the mountain by himself" (6:15). But the people came looking for Jesus and found him across the Sea of Galilee.

✍ After a brief discussion, choose one person to read this section.

Jesus knows right away what their motives are for searching him out: "You are looking for me, not because you saw signs, but because you ate your fill of the loaves" (v 26). The crowd wants to have their physical needs met, which is not surprising, because by today's standards most of the residents of Galilee would be considered very poor. Their lives were much like those of people who live in the "Two-Thirds World" today: they revolved around a daily struggle to secure food, shelter, and clothing for themselves and their families. And who wouldn't want to be near a person who could make life a little easier by providing abundant food? However, Jesus makes it clear that their vision is too narrow. Here he is offering them eternal life and all they see is a few loaves of bread. He turns the discussion to their spiritual needs: "Do not work for the food that perishes, but for the food that endures for eternal life" (v 27).

This is not the first time Jesus uses a question or comment based on limited human understanding to point to a spiritual truth. He responds similarly to Nicodemus and the woman at the well (John 3:1–21; 4:1–30). Jesus tells Nicodemus that those who enter the kingdom of God have to be born of the Spirit (3:5), responding to Nicodemus's question: "Can one enter a second time into the mother's womb and be born?" (v 4). To the woman drawing water from Jacob's well, Jesus says that he can provide living water, "a spring of water gushing up to eternal life" (4:14), using a physical substance to teach a spiritual truth.

When considered alongside Jesus's response to the devil, "One does not live by bread alone, but by every word that comes from the mouth of God" (Deut 8:3; Matt 4:4), his statement that he himself is the bread of life has even greater impact. We see that Jesus's words contain life because they are God's words. In chapter 1 we learned that the prophets of the past brought the *debar Yahweh,* the living word of God. In chapter 2 we learned that Jesus was the *Logos,* the Word, and that he was "with God, and was God" (John 1:1). In this lesson we see that his words are the words of the Father, and that they bring new life to and nurture our spiritual lives, just as bread made from grain sustains our physical lives.

▶▶▶ GOING DEEPER

Have another member read this section.

One of the most difficult things about being an embodied spirit, a spirit with a physical body, is that we pay attention to our physical, emotional, and mental needs to the neglect of our spiritual needs. In *Miracles,* C. S. Lewis discussed this estrangement of our bodies from our spirits. He wrote, "The whole conception of the New Creation involves the belief that this estrangement will be healed." He concluded that one day our spirit will ride our physical nature "so perfectly that the two together make rather a *Centaur* than a mounted knight."[2] This is what we should all strive toward—the harmonization of our spiritual nature and our physical nature until we reach the point where we can automatically do what Jesus would do.

To make progress toward this harmonization, we first must accept the fact that Jesus is our life. We may think that food is our life when we get hungry, but eating only takes care of hunger pangs for a while. It is a temporary fix. We may think that getting married will fill all our emotional needs, but anyone who has passed the newlywed stage knows this to be a falsehood. We may think that having money in the bank or a earning a PhD or being famous will fulfill our desire for security. Many stories told by the rich, educated, and famous prove this is a lie. Jesus is the only one who can bring us the spiritual food our souls desperately cry for, the only food that ultimately satisfies.

One of the primary ways this spiritual life is communicated to us is through the written Word of God, Scripture. This is where the words of God that brought the universe crashing into existence are recorded. In Scripture we learn about the plan God had for Abraham and the Israelites and ourselves before the foundations of the world were laid. In this testament to us we hear of the waywardness of a people and the prophets' perpetual call to repentance and righteousness. In the Bible we read the words of Jesus as he teaches his disciples, the crowds that come to him for nourishment, the worshipers in the temple. The Epistles record the great theological teachings of Paul, James, John, Peter, and Jude. As the written Word of God, the Bible is a record of this eternal life.

We also learn from this passage of Scripture that the kingdom of God is available now to all of those who want to enter it. Jesus made no distinctions of race or gender or social status when he was teaching. The poor were not told to sit in the back of the crowd and the rich in the front. There was no division made between farmers and city dwellers, illiterate and educated. All heard the same message that the kingdom of God was available now, not sometime in the distant future if they were lucky enough to survive the troubles and pain that came their way.

How does the Word of God help nourish your spiritual life

REFLECTION QUESTION
Allow each person a few moments to respond.

▶▶▶▶ POINTING TO GOD

Caring for our physical needs and the needs of those around us is of little use if we ignore our own and others' spiritual needs. Mother Teresa understood this lesson well. Her work in Calcutta is perhaps best exemplified by the stated mission of her organization, the Missionaries of Charity, which was to care for "the hungry, the naked, the homeless, the crippled, the blind, the lepers, all those people who feel unwanted, unloved, uncared for throughout society, people that have become a burden to the society and are shunned by everyone." These people had urgent physical needs, which she and her fellow sisters attended to as best they could. But they knew that their work encompassed more than the physical. Mother Teresa and her sisters took an eternal view of life. Often the needs of the people they served were too great, and all they could do was allow them to undergo what Mother Teresa called "a beautiful death," surrounded by people who cared for them. Mother Teresa recognized that the foundational element in this work was the spiritual. Her work and that of her sisters had to be grounded in their continuing relationship to God. She said that the only way she and her fellow sisters could carry out their work of relief amid such suffering was to lead lives "woven with prayer."[3] Not only did her relationship with God drive her work, but it also helped her to better serve the people of Calcutta because she realized that, like all of us, their greatest need was spiritual—to be cared for, loved, and recognized.

As she said in her Nobel Peace Prize acceptance speech in 1979, "And we read . . . in the Gospel very clearly—love as I have loved you—as I love

↶ Choose one member to read this section.

you—as the Father has loved me, I love you—and the harder the Father loved him, he gave him to us, and how much we love one another, we, too, must give to each other until it hurts. It is not enough for us to say: I love God, but I do not love my neighbour. St. John says you are a liar if you say you love God and you don't love your neighbour. How can you love God whom you do not see, if you do not love your neighbour whom you see, whom you touch, with whom you live. And so this is very important for us to realise that love, to be true, has to hurt. It hurt Jesus to love us, it hurt him. And to make sure we remember his great love he made himself the bread of life to satisfy our hunger for his love. Our hunger for God, because we have been created for that love. We have been created in his image. We have been created to love and be loved, and then he has become man to make it possible for us to love as he loved us. He makes himself the hungry one—the naked one—the homeless one—the sick one—the one in prison—the lonely one—the unwanted one— and he says: You did it to me. Hungry for our love, and this is the hunger of our poor people. This is the hunger that you and I must find."[4]

▶▶▶▶▶ GOING FORWARD

Have another person read this section.

It is a great challenge to Christians today to balance the physical and the spiritual. It is all too easy to become overly focused on the loud needs of the body—for food, drink, rest, clothing, and so on for our families and for ourselves. But while we don't want to become a slave to the body, neither do we want to ignore and revile it. Our body is created by God and pronounced by him to be good. Yet learning to live with Jesus means learning to harmonize our physical and spiritual natures. The only way to bring these two aspects of our existence into balance is to focus on Jesus. Yes, we need physical food, but Jesus is the food our souls crave. When our focus is on him and the Word he embodies, which we find in the Scriptures, the physical and the spiritual become perfectly harmonized. Jesus never advocated a lifestyle of strict denial; he enjoyed sharing meals with his disciples, and he honored his body with rest and care. Yet he knew that the needs of the body were nothing compared to the needs of the soul. For this reason he constantly directed our attention from physical things to our spiritual needs, needs that can be filled only by him.

And Jesus has so much more to offer us than bread to fill our stomachs. Jesus is offering us eternal life, not pie in the sky but something

LEARNING FROM JESUS

that is real and life-changing right now. When we feast on the Word, when we open ourselves to Jesus, he can teach us about this eternal view of life. This most assuredly does not mean denying our bodies—starving ourselves or locking ourselves in a closet in order to bring heaven sooner—for eternal life in the kingdom of God begins now. Once we give ourselves over to Jesus, we have the keys to the kingdom. We have access to the eternal point of view, which calls us to use our physical and spiritual natures to love and care for those around us, be they sick or homeless or hungry or heartsore. This is what Frederick Buechner means when he says that what we do "matters enormously." We can open ourselves up to Jesus and engage in kingdom work with him, or we can serve only the temporal gods of this world. When our physical and spiritual natures work in harmony—when, as Mother Teresa instructs, our actions are driven by love and interwoven with prayer—then we know that we are engaged in the work of the kingdom.

If you look critically at your life from an eternal point of view, what do you find that should be changed? What should be reprioritized?

This concludes our look at feasting on the Word. In the next chapter we will turn our attention to another avenue of learning from Jesus—confronting the powers around us.

CLOSING PRAYER

The LORD is my shepherd, I shall not want.
    He makes me lie down in green pastures;
he leads me beside still waters;
    he restores my soul.
He leads me in right paths
    for his name's sake.

Even though I walk through the darkest valley,
    I fear no evil;
for you are with me;
    your rod and your staff—
    they comfort me.

You prepare a table before me
    in the presence of my enemies;

REFLECTION QUESTION
Again, allow each member a few moments to answer this question.

↪ After everyone has had a chance to respond, the leader reads this paragraph.

↪ **Allow some time for members to encourage one another to read the Devotional and Scripture Readings and do the exercise in the following chapter before the next meeting.** Then invite the members to be silent for a few moments before leading them in reading the Closing Prayer aloud together.

At the end of the Closing Prayer, the leader asks for a volunteer to lead the next meeting.

you anoint my head with oil;
my cup overflows.
Surely goodness and mercy shall follow me
all the days of my life,
and I shall dwell in the house of the LORD
my whole life long. (PS 23)

TAKING IT FURTHER

ADDITIONAL EXERCISE

If you would like to attempt a longer fast, try fasting from lunch to lunch (skipping two meals). Do not fast from liquids, but drink water and perhaps fresh fruit juices as well. End your fast with a small meal of fresh fruit and vegetables. Try this fast once a week for several weeks. Then you will be ready for a full 24-hour fast, drinking only water. While fasting, try to focus not just on the physical reactions of your body but on the inner condition of your heart. For more, see the chapter about fasting in *Celebration of Discipline,* by Richard J. Foster.

ADDITIONAL RESOURCES

Buechner, Frederick. *The Hungering Dark.* San Francisco: HarperSan-Francisco, 1969.

Foster, Richard J. *Celebration of Discipline.* San Francisco: HarperSan-Francisco, 1978.

Muggeridge, Malcolm. *Something Beautiful for God.* San Francisco: HarperSanFrancisco, 1986.

ADDITIONAL REFLECTION QUESTIONS

In what ways has your relationship with Jesus and your study of the Bible changed your priorities, brought your life more into harmony?

In what ways might you be prioritizing the physical over the spiritual? Or vice versa?

Why is it important to harmonize the spiritual and the physical dimensions of life? What might be the dangers of emphasizing one over the other?

7 CONFRONTING THE POWERS

KEY SCRIPTURE: Mark 1:21–28; Matthew 23:1, 23–28

DEVOTIONAL READING

RICHARD J. FOSTER, *The Challenge of the Disciplined Life*

The demonic is precisely where destructive power reaches its apex. The Bible speaks of very real cosmic spiritual powers that manifest themselves in the very real structures of our very real world. The apostle Paul's favorite term to describe this spiritual reality is "the principalities and powers," though he uses other terms as well—"authorities," "dominions," "thrones," "rulers," "the elemental spirits of the universe," "princes of this world," and still others. These "powers" account for the destructive bent of power that we see all around us. Indeed, it is only as we begin to understand what the Bible calls "the principalities and powers" that we can truly confront the power issue in our own lives.

We must not dismiss this teaching as the relic of a prescientific era. The Bible is dealing with a far more profound reality than forked-tailed demons in red pajamas or benign ghosts. The powers are not spooks floating around in the air preying on unwary individuals but spiritual realities that play a definite role in the affairs of human beings.

The powers are created realities.... The powers were once related to the creative will of God; however, we no longer see them in this role. They are in revolt and rebellion against God their Creator.... The powers are incarnational. They are the energizing forces behind human beings and social structures....

The powers, however, do not "possess" just individuals but organizations and whole structures of society. Institutions can and do often become nothing more than organized sin. There are fundamental spiritual realities that underlie all political, social, and economic systems....

It is helpful for everyone to read the Devotional and Scripture Readings and do the My Life with God Exercise before the meeting. Begin the meeting with silent prayer, then move directly to Reflecting on My Life with God below.

Organizations and whole nations are often defined and controlled by particular concepts and ideologies. There is a prevailing mood or spirit that gives unity and direction to whole groups of people. These moods are not created in a vacuum, but are closely tied to very genuine spiritual realities. Hence, when we speak of "the spirit of a group" we are perhaps saying more than we know.

For example, when the Ku Klux Klan members gather together, the collective hatred is something that is greater than the sum of its parts. When a certain critical flashpoint of prejudice and ruthlessness is reached, a "mob spirit" erupts that no single individual is able to control. Spiritual powers are involved in the creation of such realities....

What does this mean to us on a practical level? Well, when we look at our own insane drive to make it to the top, we must confront the powers of pride and prestige that grip our hearts. When there is a school board decision that does a disservice to children, we must confront the powers of vested interest and self-seeking that stand behind that decision. We must seek out the "spirit" that energizes the unjust law or the unjust corporate structure and seek to defeat *it* in the power of Christ.[1]

MY LIFE WITH GOD EXERCISE

Richard Foster describes in the Devotional Reading a fundamental reality of the world we live in: although we are surrounded by creating power, power that is of God, we are also faced with destroying power, power that is demonic. When many of us hear the word *demonic,* we picture individuals affected by demons or gaining personal power through liaisons with dark forces, a view that is portrayed in popular movies like *The Exorcist* and TV shows like *Charmed* or *Buffy the Vampire Slayer*. Yet as this passage from Richard Foster shows, it is not just individuals but also organizations that are influenced and energized by demonic spiritual power. Very seldom in our culture is anything said about the "spiritual forces of evil in the heavenly places" that energize institutions (Eph 6:12c). Yet by definition these organizations, structures, and ideologies energized by demonic spiritual energy have incredible influence on our world. Such things as slavery, sexism, racism, and extreme nationalism receive their power from the demonic. And as Foster points out with the example of the Ku Klux Klan, when manifested in a group setting these evil forces are even more powerful.

LEARNING FROM JESUS

To help you understand the biblical view of demonic forces and their influence in both individual and collective affairs, read and study these Scriptures over the next few days:

Colossians 1:16 in reference to their source;
Ephesians 6:12 in reference to their nature;
Ephesians 2:2 in reference to their dominion;
Galatians 4:8–9 in reference to their worth;
1 Corinthians 2:6–8 in reference to their wisdom; and
1 Peter 5:8 in reference to their tactics.

Then, to understand the Christian response to these powers, read and study these Scriptures:

1 Corinthians 12:8–10 in reference to discernment;
1 John 4:1 in reference to testing the spirits;
Colossians 2:20–22 in reference to avoiding legalism (a stronghold of the powers);
Luke 9:24–25 in reference to overcoming narcissism (another stronghold);
Colossians 2:15 in reference to Christ defeating the powers;
Ephesians 6:10–18 in reference to our resources.

You might want to also use a concordance or a reference Bible so that you can look up related verses. After you have completed your study, spend some time seeking to discern any demonic powers that might be around you. Ask God for the wisdom to see clearly the spiritual forces, both good and evil, that are driving you and the organizations and institutions in your life.

What did you learn from studying the Scripture passages about the "principalities and powers"? What were some of the demonic spiritual powers you identified around you?

REFLECTING ON MY LIFE WITH GOD
Allow each member a few moments to answer this question.

▶ **SCRIPTURE READING:** MARK 1:21–28; MATTHEW 23:1, 23–28

They went to Capernaum; and when the sabbath came, [Jesus] entered the synagogue and taught. They were astounded at his teaching, for he taught them as one having authority, and not as the scribes. Just then there was in their synagogue a man with an unclean spirit, and he cried out, "What have you to do with us, Jesus of Nazareth? Have you come

✍ After everyone has had a chance to respond to the question, ask a member to read this passage from Scripture.

to destroy us? I know who you are, the Holy One of God." But Jesus rebuked him, saying, "Be silent, and come out of him!" And the unclean spirit, convulsing him and crying with a loud voice, came out of him. They were all amazed, and they kept on asking one another, "What is this? A new teaching—with authority! He commands even the unclean spirits, and they obey him." At once his fame began to spread throughout the surrounding region of Galilee.

Then Jesus said to the crowds and to his disciples,... "Woe to you, scribes and Pharisees, hypocrites! For you tithe mint, dill, and cummin, and have neglected the weightier matters of the law: justice and mercy and faith. It is these you ought to have practiced without neglecting the others. You blind guides! You strain out a gnat but swallow a camel!

"Woe to you, scribes and Pharisees, hypocrites! For you clean the outside of the cup and of the plate, but inside they are full of greed and self-indulgence. You blind Pharisee! First clean the inside of the cup, so that the outside also may become clean.

"Woe to you, scribes and Pharisees, hypocrites! For you are like whitewashed tombs, which on the outside look beautiful, but inside they are full of the bones of the dead and of all kinds of filth. So you also on the outside look righteous to others, but inside you are full of hypocrisy and lawlessness."

REFLECTION QUESTION
Allow each person a few moments to respond to this question.

What do the man with the unclean spirit and the Pharisees have in common? As in these two readings of Scripture, why is it that the powers of destruction—envy, rage, self-centeredness, greed—are found in our spaces for worship of God?

➤➤ GETTING THE PICTURE

After a brief discussion, choose one person to read this section.

In the two Scriptures we see Jesus confronting "cosmic powers" that manifested themselves in different ways (Eph 6:12b).

In the first passage, Jesus goes to the synagogue of the local town to worship on the Jewish Sabbath. In the service is a man possessed by a demon, and when the "unclean spirit" recognizes Jesus, it speaks to him using the man's vocal cords (see also Luke 4:33–35). Both Mark and Luke record a similar event later that day, this time in the environs of the home of Peter's mother-in-law: "As the sun was setting, all those who had any who were sick with various kinds of diseases brought them to him; and he laid his hands on each of them and cured them. Demons also came out of many, shouting, 'You are the Son of God!'" (Mark 1:34; Luke 4:40–41).

To better understand these passages, let's examine some of the numerous Gospel stories about people afflicted by demons or unclean spirits. The Gospel writers describe people afflicted with demons in different ways: "demoniac" (Matt 4:24; 8:28), "possessed with demons" (Matt 8:16; Mark 1:32), "had demons" (Luke 8:27), or had "an unclean spirit" (Mark 5:2). The persons afflicted by the demons are affected in various ways; at times they are rendered mute (Matt 9:32; Luke 11:14) or both blind and mute (Matt 12:22). According to Luke 8:2 and 8:27–30, a person can be possessed by multiple demons. In Luke 11:24–26, Jesus tells a parable of someone who was cleansed of an unclean spirit and then repossessed by the same spirit and seven more after failing to fill his spirit with the things of God. Demons are portrayed as being able to torment people (Matt 15:22), wander from place to place (Luke 11:24), and drive a person to do things they would otherwise not do (Luke 8:27). To confront demons was no small matter, but confront them Jesus does, and he defeats them soundly.

In the second Scripture we see Jesus confronting another aspect of the demonic: institutional evil. He compares the scribes and Pharisees to whitewashed tombs—outwardly pious and inwardly filthy. It was the custom of the time to whitewash tombs during Passover to warn Jews to avoid the unclean bones within them. Although outwardly pious and even calling others to share in that piety, the scribes and Pharisees as groups were energized by demonic spiritual powers manifesting themselves in religious legalism, greed, and self-indulgence. As Richard Foster writes, "Religious legalism is one of the heaviest burdens human beings ever have to bear. Jesus warns us of those who will 'bind heavy burdens, hard to bear, and lay them on men's shoulders; but they themselves will not move them with their finger' (Matt. 23:4, RSV)."[2] As we learned in the Devotional Reading, when manifested in institutions and social structures, these demonic forces grow even more powerful and influential. By confronting the legalism of the scribes and Pharisees, Jesus confronts the demonic powers that energize them.

▶▶▶ GOING DEEPER

Both passages make clear that demonic forces are a very real part of our world, affecting individuals and groups. Although many Christians

✑ Have another member read this section.

never knowingly come into direct contact with personal demons that completely possess a person, we all constantly interact with evil principalities and powers in our culture. As individuals, we need to be aware of the spirits of the world around us, the demonic influences that perpetually influence the course of events. All of us come into daily contact with institutions or governments or businesses or schools or media—like Web sites, magazines, movies, and television shows—that are clearly influenced by evil powers. These may be organizations that we learn about from TV or read about in newspapers or history books, but they could also be groups or institutions that we ourselves are part of.

Our first weapon against both the overtly demonic and more subtle powers is simply recognizing that there are evil spirits in the created order that are out to wreak havoc. Only as we acknowledge that they exist and we learn how they work can we resist their influence in our own lives and fight their influence in the public arena. As C. S. Lewis wrote in the preface to *The Screwtape Letters,* "There are two equal and opposite errors into which our race can fall about the devils. One is to disbelieve in their existence. The other is to believe, and to feel an excessive and unhealthy interest in them."[3]

Once we've recognized that evil powers do exist, our challenge is to name them and their manifestations. Of course, Jesus didn't have to recognize the unclean spirit in the first Scripture passage—it recognized him. But in the second Scripture passage, when he confronted the scribes and Pharisees, Jesus named several powers we should be on the lookout for in our own lives: greed, self-interest, and that familiar bane, legalism. Legalism is as much our enemy as is racism, sexism, and all of the other -isms that put a person in a one-up position over another person. Like these other –isms, legalism is energized by forces whose goal is to keep humans in captivity. It doesn't matter whether the legalism is well intentioned or not; many well-intentioned efforts have turned into demonic traps. Because he is at war with the good, the true, and the beautiful, Satan and his minions want to destroy humankind. And he will try to accomplish that any way he can—from harming human relationships by telling us that we are better and more deserving than those around us to encouraging us to focus on all the wrong things in life to installing murderous dictators to instigating wars of conquest. Nothing pleases Satan more than to see institutions that should be focused on doing good treating precious human beings as if they were expendable and not made in the image of God.

We also learn that it takes more than external actions to make us right with God. Projecting an image of external righteousness is another stronghold of the evil forces. It is a great temptation to care more about what others think about our piety than about the actual state of our heart. This is just another example of the demonic perverting what is good. Caring about how others perceive us is not a wrong in and of itself—what we do as Christians is a witness to those around us. The problem comes when we begin valuing our reputation as Christians more than our actual relationship with God. So it is with sex, money, and self-interest; all can be perverted by the evil cosmic forces around us. The scribes and Pharisees had concentrated on right actions for decades, but Jesus declared that their tithes of the smallest seeds, rigorous rules for cleanliness, and impeccable dress were not sufficient. In the Scripture passage, Jesus doesn't explicitly say that right actions come from a heart turned toward God. He didn't need to. The image he uses says it: "First clean the inside of the cup." And how do we become clean on the inside? By constant attention to our relationship with the Lord through the practice of such Spiritual Disciplines as prayer and worship and confession. When our hearts are right with the Lord, right actions will automatically follow. In this way we will be formed to avoid the self-centeredness, ignorance, self-protection, and narcissism through which unredeemed principalities and powers use us and our social groupings to promote and perpetuate a satanic vision for the world.

In what ways do we as individuals and institutions make ourselves vulnerable to the demonic influences in the world around us?

REFLECTION QUESTION
Allow each person a few moments to respond.

▶▶▶▶ POINTING TO GOD

Of all the institutional evils throughout history that could be considered to be demonically influenced, most of us would put slavery at the top of the list. Yet it was an accepted part of life until relatively recently. Those Christians who fought against this deeply embedded institutional power should be counted among our religious heroes. One of these was William Wilberforce, who during the late eighteenth and early nineteenth centuries helped lead British Parliament in banning the slave trade. Wilberforce became an evangelical Christian early in his parliamentary career and was inspired by his faith to turn his attention to matters of social reform, such as factory working conditions and housing. An acquaintance, Lady Middleton, approached Wilberforce and persuaded him to use his influence in Parliament to pass a ban on the slave trade.

Choose one member to read this section.

He was unsure of his own powers in the area. "I feel the great importance of the subject and I think myself unequal to the task allotted to me," he wrote. But he overcame his apprehension and made his first anti-slave trade speech in 1789.

It took until 1807, but a law was finally passed that made it illegal for any English citizen to transport a slave. Wilberforce was credited as a major force in the law's creation. The fight was not yet over, though. Slavery was not yet illegal, only the transport of slaves. Slave traders were fined one hundred pounds for every slave found on their ships, so they avoided the problem by throwing the slaves overboard if they feared discovery by the British navy. Even after he retired from Parliament, Wilberforce continued to work for the freedom of slaves until his death in 1833. Just a month later, the Slavery Abolition Act freed all slaves in the British Empire, from the Americas to Eastern Asia.

William Wilberforce always said that his work in this area stemmed from his Christian faith. As he wrote in his diary in 1787, "God Almighty has set before me two great objects, the suppression of the Slave Trade and the Reformation of Manners" [i.e., morals].

▶▶▶▶▶ GOING FORWARD

Have another person read this section.

William Wilberforce was truly an example of Ephesians 5:11: "Take no part in the unfruitful works of darkness, but instead expose them." He used the creating power he had as a member of Parliament to confront the destroying power of the slave trade. We too encounter organizations and institutions that are energized by the demonic. And like Wilberforce, we need to confront them. Richard Foster lays out a way to do this in *The Challenge of the Disciplined Life*. Our first task is discernment. We ask God to help us see the demonic forces energizing the institutions and the world around us, including those forces that may have a hold in our own lives. Next we name the powers—whether they be narcissism, religious legalism, racism, or greed—and face those powers that are tempting us. As Foster puts it, "Right at the outset, we all need to see and to address the powers that nip at our own heels. Otherwise we will utilize the tactics of the very powers we oppose and, in the end, become as evil as they. We must look squarely into the face of our own greed and lust for power and see them for what they are."[4]

Along these same lines, we can confront and defeat these powers by renouncing the things that the powers use against us. When we can stop caring about our possessions, our reputation, and the other things this world holds dear, then we leave the evil forces of this world nothing with which to threaten us. Next, we defeat the powers by refusing to use the weapons of the powers of this world—domination, control, manipulation. Instead we use the resources we have been given by God, those weapons of Ephesians 6:10–18—truth, righteousness, peace, faith, salvation, the Word of God, and prayer. The power of these resources cannot be overestimated. They measure up over and against any of the weapons of this world.

Throughout, we rely on the help of the Holy Spirit. We also remember that Christ has already soundly defeated these powers with his death and resurrection. As Colossians 2:15 tells us, "He disarmed the rulers and authorities and made a public example of them, triumphing over them in it."

How have you overcome destructive powers in your life? What are some powers you still must work to defeat?

REFLECTION QUESTION
Again, allow each member a few moments to answer this question.

This concludes our look at confronting the powers. In the next chapter we will turn our attention to another avenue of learning from Jesus—how Jesus welcomes us into community.

After everyone has had a chance to respond, the leader reads this paragraph.

Allow some time for members to encourage one another to read the Devotional and Scripture Readings and do the exercise in the following chapter before the next meeting. Then invite the members to be silent for a few moments before leading them in reading the Closing Prayer aloud together.

CLOSING PRAYER

The LORD is my shepherd, I shall not want.
    He makes me lie down in green pastures;
he leads me beside still waters;
    he restores my soul.
He leads me in right paths
    for his name's sake.

Even though I walk through the darkest valley,
    I fear no evil;
for you are with me;
      your rod and your staff—
      they comfort me.

You prepare a table before me
    in the presence of my enemies;
you anoint my head with oil;
    my cup overflows.

⤸ At the end of the Closing Prayer, the leader asks for a volunteer to lead the next meeting.

Surely goodness and mercy shall follow me
 all the days of my life,
and I shall dwell in the house of the LORD
 my whole life long. (PS 23)

TAKING IT FURTHER

ADDITIONAL EXERCISE

Many Christian authors have written novels about spiritual warfare. Read (or reread) a classic of this genre, C. S. Lewis's *Screwtape Letters*, and a more contemporary novel, Frank Peretti's *This Present Darkness*. Contrast the view each presents of the spiritual warfare occurring around us and the temptations facing us. What do the two books share in their portrayals of the principalities and powers around us? Which corresponds most closely to your own experience?

ADDITIONAL RESOURCES

Foster, Richard J. *The Challenge of the Disciplined Life*. San Francisco: HarperSanFrancisco, 1985.

"Hitler and the Occult," *In Search of History*, DVD or VHS (New York: A & E Television Network, n.d.), available from *http://store.aetv.com*.

Peck, M. Scott. *People of the Lie*. New York: Simon & Schuster/ Touchstone, 1998.

Wimber, John. *Power Healing*. San Francisco: HarperSanFrancisco, 1991.

Wink, Walter. *Naming the Powers*. Philadelphia, PA: Fortress, 1984.

ADDITIONAL REFLECTION QUESTIONS

C. S. Lewis wrote that it was a mistake either to ignore demons or to take an excessive interest in them. Which side do you tend to err on and why?

What do you think is the greatest institutional evil in today's world?

How can we guard against the evil powers in our groups, companies, and communities?

WELCOMING US INTO COMMUNITY

8

DEVOTIONAL READING

DIETRICH BONHOEFFER, *Life Together*

The physical presence of other Christians is a source of incomparable joy and strength to the believer. Longingly, the imprisoned apostle Paul calls his "dearly beloved son in the faith," Timothy, to come to him in prison in the last days of his life; he would see him again and have him near. Paul has not forgotten the tears Timothy shed when last they parted (II Tim. 1:4). Remembering the congregation in Thessalonica, Paul prays "night and day ... exceedingly that we might see your face" (I Thess. 3:10). The aged John knows that his joy will not be full until he can come to his own people and speak face to face instead of writing with ink (II John 12).

It is helpful for everyone to read the Devotional and Scripture Readings and do the My Life with God Exercise before the meeting. Begin the meeting with silent prayer, then move directly to Reflecting on My Life with God below.

The believer feels no shame, as though he were still living too much in the flesh, when he yearns for the physical presence of other Christians. Man was created a body, the Son of God appeared on earth in the body, he was raised in the body, in the sacrament the believer receives the Lord Christ in the body, and the resurrection of the dead will bring about the perfected fellowship of God's spiritual-physical creatures. The believer therefore lauds the Creator, the Redeemer, God, Father, Son and Holy Spirit, for the bodily presence of a brother. The prisoner, the sick person, the Christian in exile sees in the companionship of a fellow Christian a physical sign of the gracious presence of the triune God. Visitor and visited in loneliness recognize in each other the Christ who is present in the body; they receive and meet each other as one meets the Lord, in reverence, humility, and joy. They receive each other's benedictions as the benediction of the Lord Jesus Christ. But if there is so much blessing and joy even in a single encounter of brother with brother, how inexhaustible are the riches that open up for those who by God's will are privileged to live in the daily fellowship of life with other Christians! ...

Christianity means community through Jesus Christ and in Jesus Christ. No Christian community is more or less than this. Whether it be a brief, single encounter or the daily fellowship of years, Christian community is only this. We belong to one another only through and in Jesus Christ.

What does this mean? It means, first, that a Christian needs others because of Jesus Christ. It means, second, that a Christian comes to others only through Jesus Christ. It means, third, that in Jesus Christ we have been chosen from eternity, accepted in time, and united for eternity.[1]

MY LIFE WITH GOD EXERCISE

In this chapter we will look more closely at what Jesus has to teach us about Christianity as community. Many of us who have grown up in or been associated with the church in the United States would most likely define Christianity as a personal belief in Jesus Christ as our Savior, failing to mention the community aspect that Dietrich Bonhoeffer highlights when he defines Christianity as a "community through Jesus Christ and in Jesus Christ." We know that this aspect of the Christian life was at the forefront of Dietrich Bonhoeffer's mind at the time he wrote *Life Together* because the underground seminary established by the German Confessing Church at Finkenwalde, where he had taught and lived, had just been closed by the Nazi Gestapo. Unique to the seminary was the "Bruderhaus," or House of Brothers, a community for single men who pledged to live and work together, sharing a commitment to a simple lifestyle and to shared rituals, including morning worship, prayers and readings, personal confession, and mutual encouragement. The express purpose of the community was to prepare its members for outside service.

As Bonhoeffer explains, community is a necessity for all Christians: "God has willed that we should seek and find His living Word in the witness of a brother, in the mouth of man. Therefore, the Christian needs another Christian who speaks God's Word to Him. He needs him again and again when he becomes uncertain and discouraged, for by himself he cannot help himself without belying the truth. He needs his brother man as a bearer and proclaimer of the divine word of salvation. He needs his brother solely because of Jesus Christ. The Christ in his own heart is weaker than the Christ in the word of his brother; his own heart is uncertain, his brother's is sure."[2]

Although we all experience some level of Christian community or fellowship, perhaps in a Bible study group, church services, community outreach, or choir, likely very few of us have lived in a Christian community like Finkenwalde. Prayerfully try to imagine what it would be like to live in an explicitly Christian community. You may have lived in a dormitory or fraternity or sorority during college that had its own rules and regulations. Unless it was Christian, those rules were probably nothing like the disciplines practiced by the students at Finkenwalde, but they do lay a foundation for this exercise. As you imagine what it would be like, write down the advantages and disadvantages of living in close proximity to other Christians day after day. You might want to consider the activities in which the residents of Finkenwalde were expected to participate plus any others you might think of.

Once you have imagined what it would be like to live in an intentional Christian community, consider the different kinds of Christian community in your life. Where do you find fellowship, both within and outside the church? Make another list describing the community you experience. You may want to consider periods of your life during which you experienced more or less Christian community and fellowship, as well as the present. Compare your list to the list you created about the disadvantages and advantages of living in a community such as Finkenwalde. Which aspects of community are in your life? Which are missing? What are some ways you can promote fellowship like that described by Bonhoeffer? This week pay special attention to the ways you experience fellowship. Plan extra time with friends or consider attending a church service or fellowship group that you don't normally participate in. If you found that personal confession was lacking in your life, consider asking a trusted friend to hear your confession and pray with you about it. You might also want to look at Gospel accounts of how Jesus celebrated community with his disciples and the others around him—attending weddings, sharing meals, and so on.

What did you learn about an intentional Christian community as you were imagining what it would be like to live in one? About the level of community in your own life?

REFLECTING ON MY LIFE WITH GOD
Allow each member a few moments to answer this question.

➤ SCRIPTURE READING: LUKE 15:1–10

Now all the tax collectors and sinners were coming near to listen to him. And the Pharisees and the scribes were grumbling and saying, "This fellow welcomes sinners and eats with them."

After everyone has had a chance to respond to the question, ask a member to read this passage from Scripture.

So he told them this parable: "Which one of you, having a hundred sheep and losing one of them, does not leave the ninety-nine in the wilderness and go after the one that is lost until he finds it? When he has found it, he lays it on his shoulders and rejoices. And when he comes home, he calls together his friends and neighbors, saying to them, 'Rejoice with me, for I have found my sheep that was lost.' Just so, I tell you, there will be more joy in heaven over one sinner who repents than over ninety-nine righteous persons who need no repentance.

"Or what woman having ten silver coins, if she loses one of them, does not light a lamp, sweep the house, and search carefully until she finds it? When she has found it, she calls together her friends and neighbors, saying, 'Rejoice with me, for I have found the coin that I had lost.' Just so, I tell you, there is joy in the presence of the angels of God over one sinner who repents."

REFLECTION QUESTION
Allow each person a few moments to respond to this question.

What is your reaction to these parables? Do you find yourself relating more to the lost sheep or the ninety-nine righteous persons? Why?

▶▶ GETTING THE PICTURE

✒ After a brief discussion, choose one person to read this section.

The parables of the lost sheep and the lost coin are part of a trilogy; the last is the parable of the Prodigal Son, one that many of us know well. Though similar, the parables describe three different kinds of people: those who wander away from their community, those who get left behind by their community, and those who leave of their own free will. All three emphasize God's concern for each member of the People of God and describe the celebration when the lost ones are found or come home. Perhaps a little background on sheep will help us better understand the first parable.

The lost sheep in the parable may well have been what shepherds call a "cast" sheep. Sometimes when sheep wander away and lie down to rest, they may lie next to a little depression and roll over onto their sides a little too far, causing all four feet to come off of the ground. The more they struggle, the farther they roll over onto their backs, until their feet are sticking up and waving around like flags. If the shepherd doesn't see the sheep get into trouble or fails to count the flock periodically, he might not miss the sheep until that evening when he counts them as they enter the pen or fold. Shutting the gate firmly to keep the rest of the flock safe, he must go back into the fields where the sheep grazed that day. When he finds the cast sheep, sometimes by listening for its frantic bleating, he gently rolls it back onto its belly so it can get up. Sometimes the sheep's legs have been in the air so long its circulation is impaired and the shepherd must gently massage them until the circulation is restored. Then, once the sheep is able to walk on its own, together they return to the fold. In the parable the shepherd carries the sheep back to the fold with great relief and calls for a celebration.

As we read the parable of the lost coin, we need to remember that many people were poor in Jesus's culture. A common coin of that time, the denarius, was worth a day's work and was about the size of a U.S. or Canadian dime. The smallest denomination was the mite, which was about a half inch in diameter and worth only a fraction of a modern penny. Because the woman was so concerned about its loss, we can surmise that the lost coin was worth far more than a mite. For a woman to lose one coin would have been an emergency. The loss could have meant the difference between having ample food for her family to eat or making food meant to sustain them for just nine days last for ten. No wonder Jesus tells us that there was rejoicing in the neighborhood when she found it.

▶▶▶ GOING DEEPER

The context for these parables was another confrontation between Jesus and the scribes and Pharisees, the two groups who were monitoring what Jesus was doing. The fact that they were grumbling about Jesus welcoming and eating with "sinners" highlights just how important it was to the scribes and Pharisees to divide people into groups of "in" and "out," "clean" and "unclean." In their defense, under Mosaic law, eating practices were carefully delineated: sharing a meal with someone who was unclean was a serious violation in their eyes. But this passage is another example of the religious leaders not only focusing on the letter of the law rather than the spirit but also trying to force everyone to conform to their own interpretation of the Mosaic law and oral tradition. In the process they were forcing people who had been born into the Jewish community and faith out of relationship with their ethnicity and blessed status as members of the People of God. This leads us to observe several principles about what God values.

In the kingdom of God, all members of the community are precious and irreplaceable. In a culture based on agriculture and raising animals,

✍ Have another member read this section.

each sheep is precious. The coin was precious to the woman who lost it, not because of what it was—a piece of metal—but because it could buy things needed to sustain the life and well-being of her family. And who can place a value on a child who has gone astray?

We also notice that all of these lost things (the sheep, the coin, and the son) were meant for very good reasons to be part of a larger grouping. The sheep belonged to a large flock. The coin had been nestled among nine other coins. The Prodigal Son had been part of a family. All communities of one sort or another, all of which had lost a member. The sheep had wandered away and, because of its physical limitations, had probably become cast. Perhaps the woman had been careless, and a coin had slipped out of her bag or been dropped and had rolled into a crack or under something. The Prodigal Son had left his family of his own volition. All were lost to the community of which they were a part, and the community was not complete without them.

Like the scribes and the Pharisees, too often we try to divide people into categories of "us" and "them," "sinners" and "non-sinners," "Christians" and "non-Christians," or perhaps "good Christians" and "not-so-good Christians." We have to remember that we do not always know what is in others' hearts. Trying to fit people into the pattern we think is best for them is a constant danger. One of the mysteries of human nature is that we believe we should have the freedom to be the person God intended us to be, but we're unwilling to allow God to work with others the same way. We are constantly trying to impose our way of thinking, our way of doing things, our way of life onto them. But what we're really saying is that we do not trust God to do his work in their life without our input.

God does not call us to close the borders of our community; rather we are to welcome any and all to join us in God's kingdom work. We are to be ambassadors of community. That means we should seek out and welcome not only those who have never been part of our Christian community but also those people who have left. It doesn't matter if they left because of circumstances beyond their control or of their own free will. Nor does it matter if they left because they were hurt or bored. When a person leaves the community, he or she leaves behind a vacancy that damages the community.

REFLECTION QUESTION
Allow each person a few moments to respond.

Have you ever been hurt by someone who unfairly labeled you a sinner or a not-so-good Christian? What are some ways in which you tend to divide people into "us" and "them," try to force people to conform to your way of doing things?

LEARNING FROM JESUS

▸▸▸ POINTING TO GOD

Although there have been many communities and orders throughout Christian history, the Taizé community founded by Brother Roger is especially notable for its commitment to inclusivity. Brother Roger's international Taizé movement is named for the small village in France where the young Protestant pastor set up a community shortly after World War II. He and three friends started the community by taking three vows: celibacy, communal sharing of goods, and acceptance of an authority. Eventually the community came to include Roman Catholic brothers as well as brothers from the Reformed Churches, making it the world's first truly ecumenical community.[3] Their aim then and now is to be a living sign of hope, a sign of the unity of the Church.

✍ Choose one member to read this section.

Through common prayer, a monastic lifestyle, and a commitment to service, Brother Roger called the Brothers of Taizé to "bear the burdens of others, accept whatever hurts each day brings, so that you are concretely in communion with the sufferings of Christ: there lies our main discipline. Never stand still, advance with your brothers, race towards the goal in the steps of Christ. Be a sign for others of joy and brotherly love."[4] But one doesn't have to be a formally declared brother to be welcomed into the life of the community. Visitors are frequent; they are encouraged to spend at least a week with the community to share in prayer and the celebration of the liturgy. Since the visitors, like the brothers themselves, are from all over the world, they then bring Taizé's message of unity and reconciliation back to their own homes and churches. As is written in many different languages in the Church of Reconciliation at Taizé, "Let all who enter here be reconciled, brother with brother, sister with sister, nation with nation."[5]

▸▸▸▸▸ GOING FORWARD

The Renovaré Spiritual Formation Bible reminds us, "The aim of God in history is the creation of an all-inclusive community of loving persons with God himself at the very center of this community as its prime Sustainer and most glorious Inhabitant (Eph 2:19–22; 3:10). The Bible traces the formation of this community from the creation in the Garden of Eden all the way to the new heaven and the new earth."[6] We can also see from Jesus's teachings and from the experiences and wisdom of Dietrich Bonhoeffer and Brother Roger just how central community is to

✍ Have another person read this section.

Christian life. Community is the place where we celebrate, pray, confess, and are challenged. We enjoy community in a variety of ways—through weddings, worship, shared meals, and simply time spent together. At its heart, community is the body of Christ. It is knowing that we all have an indispensable role in the kingdom of God and that we can best accomplish God's work by working together. It is in the context of the community that God is best able to shape us, as we learn from and teach those around us, always cautious that we are not just imposing our way of doing things onto others. We are made for community.

But perhaps the most important word in the above quotation is "all-inclusive." As Brother Roger demonstrated in the Taizé community, God's kingdom is meant for everyone. Thus, just as Jesus welcomes us into the community of the kingdom of God, we must always seek to welcome others into our community. We also mourn the loss of even one person, for every member is "for building up the body of Christ" (Eph 4:12).

REFLECTION QUESTION
Again, allow each member a few moments to answer this question.

Who in your life is outside the community? How can you welcome him, her, or them back into fellowship?

🕊 After everyone has had a chance to respond, the leader reads this paragraph.

This concludes our look at how Jesus welcomes us into community. In the next chapter we will turn our attention to another avenue of learning from Jesus—living out God's abundance.

🕊 **Allow some time for members to encourage one another to read the Devotional and Scripture Readings and do the exercise in the following chapter before the next meeting.** Then invite the members to be silent for a few moments before leading them in reading the Closing Prayer aloud together.

CLOSING PRAYER

The LORD is my shepherd, I shall not want.
    He makes me lie down in green pastures;
he leads me beside still waters;
    he restores my soul.
He leads me in right paths
    for his name's sake.

Even though I walk through the darkest valley,
    I fear no evil;
for you are with me;
    your rod and your staff—
    they comfort me.

You prepare a table before me
    in the presence of my enemies;

you anoint my head with oil;
  my cup overflows.
Surely goodness and mercy shall follow me
  all the days of my life,
and I shall dwell in the house of the LORD
  my whole life long. (PS 23)

✍ At the end of the Closing Prayer, the leader asks for a volunteer to lead the next meeting.

TAKING IT FURTHER

- If you have never before attended a Taizé-style service, check your local newspaper or the Internet to find a Taizé service to attend in a nearby church.

ADDITIONAL EXERCISES

- Read the Parable of the Prodigal Son (Luke 15:11–32). With whom do you most identify? The father? The older son? The younger son? How could the primary characters have acted differently at various points to encourage community and redeem their relationships?

Bonhoeffer, Dietrich. *Life Together*. San Francisco: HarperSanFrancisco, 1954.

Brother Roger. *The Parable of Community: The Rule and Other Basic Texts of Taizé*. New York: Seabury, 1981.

Vanier, Jean. *Community and Growth*. Mahwah, NJ: Paulist, 1989.

ADDITIONAL RESOURCES

Were you ever a lost sheep, outside the Christian community? Explain.

ADDITIONAL REFLECTION QUESTIONS

How well does your church seek to bring in and welcome lost sheep? What is your role?

What can you do to continue to promote community among those with whom you already have a relationship or fellowship?

LIVING ABUNDANCE

KEY SCRIPTURE: Mark 6:30–44

DEVOTIONAL READING

WALTER BRUEGGEMANN, "Enough Is Enough"

The Bible is about abundance. From the first chapters of Genesis, God not only initiates abundance—calling forth plants and fish and birds and animals—but promises continued abundance by commanding them to "increase and multiply" (1:22). God's generosity and fidelity reach their climax on the sixth day, when God proclaims a sufficiency for "everything that has the breath of life" and declares all this "very good" (1:30–31). Having thus set in motion a world of abundance, God rests—the mechanisms are in place, the world will have enough.

Of course, things don't turn out quite that way. Dissatisfied with what they've been given, God's creatures want more. Instead, they get less. The bountiful earth becomes stingy; even bread won't abound without sweat. Scarcity sets in, bubbling under the narrative, breaking through here and there, and finally bursting forth full-blown in Egypt, where abundance gets locked up in Pharaoh's warehouses, to be parceled out for money, then possessions, then slavery. Scarcity reaches a point where the immigrant Israelites, having traded their freedom for food, don't even have straw to make the bricks that slavery demands. Like so many other victims of scarcity, they cry out—whether for help, or just from the hurt, the Bible doesn't say.

God hears their cry, and sends Moses to tell Pharaoh that the God of abundance has come to free the Israelites from this ideology of scarcity. And Yahweh won't accept no for an answer. It takes convincing, but Pharaoh finally agrees—at least long enough for the Israelites to gather their belongings and put a river between themselves and Egypt.

> It is helpful for everyone to read the Devotional and Scripture Readings and do the My Life with God Exercise before the meeting. Begin the meeting with silent prayer, then move directly to Reflecting on My Life with God below.

It isn't long before what they have left behind starts to look good compared to what they must face. They left the land of scarcity thinking they would bounce into the land of abundance. Instead, they find themselves at risk in a wilderness, a desert with no visible life-support systems, a place of scarcity where even bread seems an impossibility. Having inhaled the continuing reality of scarcity throughout their lives, the Israelites breathe out murmurs, complaints, condemnations, and reveries of Egypt—where at least there was bread.

Then, in this desert wilderness, bread inexplicably appears. A fine, flaky substance comes down, answering Israel's risk with a manifestation of God's faithful generosity. This bread violates all their categories: It overturns their conviction about scarcity and cancels their anxiety about hunger. The gift of bread transforms the wilderness. And from that point on, Israel would entertain the thought that a place of perceived scarcity may turn out to be a place of wondrous abundance.

In the New Testament, Jesus knows all about the generosity and fidelity of God. In his very person, the whole of Israel's faith is expressed with a new intensity. Filled with God's generosity, Jesus went around to people suffering from scarcity—of health, of acceptance, of power, of understanding—and replaced it with a gift of abundance.

The eighth chapter of Mark's Gospel contains the second feeding narrative, a story rich in Israel's past. Jesus notices that the people who've been listening to him have run out of food. He's been here before, back in chapter six where he fed the five thousand. But hunger—scarcity—isn't a one-time experience, and Jesus isn't in the "symbolic gesture" business. He's in the generosity business, and that means being constantly alert to any mismatch between the generosity of God and the needs of the people.

In this instance, the mismatch moves Jesus "to compassion"—a Greek term that means that his insides are turned over. Jesus has this strange bodily sense of an emergency. He cares about the hungry and knows something must be done....

Mark uses four words to describe what Jesus did: took, gave thanks, broke, and gave. The words are familiar; they are Eucharistic words. Out in the desert, Jesus uses seven loaves to conduct a sit-down thanksgiving dinner that matches the needs of the people with the generosity of God. And his actions are transformative.... Jesus has put into practice the generosity of the Creator. It is as though Genesis 1 reappears in Mark 8, and the world is again made new.[1]

MY LIFE WITH GOD EXERCISE

At the beginning of the quoted article, Brueggemann writes, "[The] peculiar thing, at least from a biblical perspective, is that the rich—the ones with the abundance—rely on an ideology of scarcity, while the poor—the ones suffering from scarcity—rely on an ideology of abundance." He further explains that when we operate from an ideology of scarcity we hold on to what we have, hoard it, put it aside for a rainy day. People who operate from an ideology of abundance do just the opposite. They "are willing to have but not hoard," knowing that "there will even be more than enough left over."[2]

Brueggemann's teaching strikes at the heart of our materialistic culture, in which we determine who is important by their gross income or net worth. Lists of the richest people are made and constantly revised. Although we may outwardly revile statements like that made by banker J. P. Morgan ("How much is enough?" he is asked; "Just a little bit more," he replies), we all secretly or not so secretly desire to be rich in money and possessions.

"No one can serve two masters; for a slave will either hate the one and love the other, or be devoted to the one and despise the other. You cannot serve God and wealth," Jesus teaches us (Matt 6:24). Wealth is a rival god. And because there is only so much of it to go around at any given time and we crave the security it brings, this god takes hold of our hearts, and wealth—not God—becomes our master.

Do I live my life out of an ideology of scarcity or abundance? If it's out of an ideology of scarcity, why is that? Does wealth have a hold on my heart I have yet to break? How do I break *mammon*'s hold on me? Questions like these, and more, should trouble our minds and hearts, if they do not already.

Because most of us fall into the group of those who operate from an ideology of scarcity, we need to work on overcoming our addiction to wealth and possessions. And for those of us who feel we are operating from an ideology of abundance, it is always good to consider the issue and review the biblical teachings. Before the next meeting, study and meditate on these Scriptures, making sure to ask the Lord to open your heart to their teaching before you begin: Psalm 49:10–11; Proverbs 18:11; Matthew 6:19–21; Mark 4:18–19, 10:23–27; and Luke 16:10–13. At the end of your study and meditation, choose one thing that you prize and give it away. Try to give it to someone you don't know. A local charitable organization can help you find a person or family and will be able to tell you what things they need. Before, during, and afterward, monitor your feelings. Did you feel sad? Joyful? Remorseful? Resentful? Indifferent?

What did you learn about your attitude toward material things?

REFLECTING ON MY LIFE WITH GOD
Allow each member a few moments to answer this question.

✍ After everyone has had a chance to respond to the question, ask a member to read this passage from Scripture.

➤ SCRIPTURE READING: MARK 6:30–44

The apostles gathered around Jesus, and told him all that they had done and taught. He said to them, "Come away to a deserted place all by yourselves and rest a while." For many were coming and going, and they had no leisure even to eat. And they went away in the boat to a deserted place by themselves. Now many saw them going and recognized them, and they hurried there on foot from all the towns and arrived ahead of them. As he went ashore, he saw a great crowd; and he had compassion for them, because they were like sheep without a shepherd; and he began to teach them many things. When it grew late, his disciples came to him and said, "This is a deserted place, and the hour is now very late; send them away so that they may go into the surrounding country and villages and buy something for themselves to eat." But he answered them, "You give them something to eat." They said to him, "Are we to go and buy two hundred denarii worth of bread, and give it to them to eat?" And he said to them, "How many loaves have you? Go and see." When they had found out, they said, "Five, and two fish." Then he ordered them to get all the people to sit down in groups on the green grass. So they sat down in groups of hundreds and of fifties. Taking the five loaves and the two fish, he looked up to heaven, and blessed and broke the loaves, and gave them to his disciples to set before the people; and he divided the two fish among them all. And all ate and were filled; and they took up twelve baskets full of broken pieces and of the fish. Those who had eaten the loaves numbered five thousand men.

What would you think of Jesus had you been in the crowd that was fed?

REFLECTION QUESTION
Allow each person a few moments to respond to this question.

✍ After a brief discussion, choose one person to read this section.

➤➤ GETTING THE PICTURE

One of the first things we notice about this passage is that it is set in a deserted location. The locale immediately recalls one of God's early demonstrations of abundance: manna falling from the sky for the Israelites, who were wandering the desert in search of the Promised Land. As Walter Brueggemann wrote in the Devotional Reading, the manna was yet another "manifestation of God's faithful generosity." The process of gathering, eating, and storing the manna was an important lesson in the theology of abundance. Everyone had just enough. Exodus 16:18 reads, "But when they measured [the manna] with an omer, those who gathered much had nothing over, and those who gathered little had no shortage; they gathered as much as each of them needed." And when anyone tried to hoard some of the manna until the next day, it became foul and unfit to eat. There was enough for the day (and two days' worth before the Sabbath) and no more. Here in the Scripture Reading, in another deserted place, God provides enough for everyone. We see clear parallels between God's provision of manna and this story, parallels that would not have been lost on Jesus's Jewish audience.

We learn that by the time of the feeding of the five thousand, Jesus's fame has spread around Galilee. People have heard of the healings he has performed, the demons he has cast out, and the teachings he and his disciples are spreading. This fame seems to have made for a crowded and uncomfortable atmosphere around Jesus and his disciples. Mark tells us that "many were coming and going and they had no leisure even to eat" (v 31). It is no wonder that Jesus instructs the disciples to come away with him to a deserted place. But the crowd is so eager to hear what Jesus has to say that they follow them. It is hard to imagine that Jesus was pleased about the arrival of the crowd. He had just been reunited with his disciples after sending them out to preach, heal, and cast out demons. We can assume that when he leads them out to the deserted place he is looking forward to spending time with them as well as enjoying some much-needed rest and solitude. The verses immediately preceding this passage describe the death of his cousin John the Baptist, so it is also possible that Jesus desired some time alone with the disciples to mourn his death.

Yet Jesus reacts to the crowd not with anger but with that wonderful word: "compassion." He recognizes their hunger—both spiritual and physical—and responds with abundance: the teachings he offers for their spiritual hunger, and the food he multiplies for their physical hunger.

▶▶▶ GOING DEEPER

The first and primary spiritual formation principle we take away from this passage is that Jesus is the source of abundance. Jesus saw a need in the

Have another member read this section.

crowd before him and was quick to respond with abundance. He does the same with us. He is the vine and we are the branches (John 15:1–5). When we trust in him, we can expect that he will meet our spiritual and physical needs. This is a message repeated throughout the New Testament. Philippians 4:19 states, "And my God will fully satisfy every need of yours according to his riches in glory in Christ Jesus."

We also see that just as Jesus gives us abundance, so we should share what we have with others. Too often we are like the disciples. We are cautious; we hoard any extra for ourselves and our family. We think we do not have enough to share, enough to go around. Yet Jesus teaches us the amazing lesson that we can do more than we think with what we have at our disposal. The disciples couldn't see any way that the measly amount of food they had could feed all the hungry people. Yet it did. If we all share what we have, there is enough. What a teaching in today's world of ever-growing disparity between rich and poor. Imagine the change in our world if we all took this teaching to heart. It is easy to say that there is no way we can make a difference, but we all have gifts we can share. We are to show generosity not just with our material possessions and our wealth but with our time and spiritual gifts.

Another lesson we find here is the importance of community, of gathering together to break bread. Although the disciples made the reasonable suggestion that Jesus should pause in his teaching to let the people go find food in neighboring towns, Jesus did not dismiss the crowd. Instead he instructed them to gather together in groups of fifties and hundreds to eat together on the grass. This type of shared fellowship is a consistent theme in Jesus's life. Although he sometimes went off alone to pray, he spent most of his time in community with his disciples. Neither can we be Christians in a vacuum. We have a need for community, to remember God together, to learn from each other, to challenge and encourage each other.

Finally, we learn to thank God for the abundance he showers upon us. In this passage we see Jesus do what he did so many other times in the Gospels—he blessed the food, broke it, and gave thanks. We can almost imagine the disciples watching with open mouths, most likely thinking, "What is he doing giving thanks for that food, which isn't nearly enough? We're going to have a riot on our hands!" Yet Jesus gave thanks anyway, and the food was enough. Like Jesus, we should thank God for all that we have. Even when we think we don't have nearly enough—enough food, enough health, enough money, enough perseverance, enough happiness, enough faith—we can always thank God for what we do have. For the miracles continue. Thanking God for our faith has a way of strengthening it; thanking God for our health has a way of making us feel stronger; thanking God for our happiness has a way of brightening our perspectives on life. The abundance continues.

In what ways has God blessed you with abundance?

REFLECTION QUESTION
Allow each person a few moments to respond.

▶▶▶ POINTING TO GOD

Dorothy Day put these words about living in abundance into practice. As a young reporter in New York City during the Great Depression of the 1930s, she reported on issues of social justice. When she was baptized as a Catholic at age thirty, she went about this work with a renewed sense of purpose. After reporting on a hunger strike in Washington, D.C., staged by poor people agitating for work, she went to a local church and "offered up a special prayer, a prayer which came with tears and with anguish, that some way would open up for me to use what talents I possessed for my fellow workers, for the poor."[3] She soon met Peter Maurin, with whose help she was able to meet the goal for which she had prayed. The two committed themselves to helping the poor, founding a newspaper called *The Catholic Worker* in which they wrote about Catholic social teachings, and establishing houses of hospitality where the poor could come to get food and rest. Dorothy Day faithfully practiced the theology of abundance. She gave all of her resources—her time, money, energy, and prayers—to her work for the poor. She said, "The best things to do with the best things in life is to give them up."[4]

Richard Foster describes Dorothy Day and her commitment to abundant life for all as a "living reproach": "Her radical identification with the poor, her vigorous championing of the cause of the worker, her works of mercy to the homeless, her willingness to be spent in the cause of Christ—all stand as a living reproach to we who are 'at ease in Zion.'"[5]

✍ Choose one member to read this section.

▶▶▶▶ GOING FORWARD

In John 15:1–2, Jesus says, "I am the true vine, and my Father is the vinegrower. He removes every branch in me that bears no fruit. Every branch that bears fruit he prunes to make it bear more fruit." Jesus gives us life; we are the branches that are nourished by him and pruned by the Father. This glorious abundance we receive in Jesus is not, however, to stop with us. We are called to share what we have with others, to practice

✍ Have another person read this section.

an ideology of abundance rather than an ideology of scarcity. This entails giving freely and not hoarding our resources. Time and time again Jesus calls us not to value our material possessions. This is a hard lesson for us today. It is difficult to resist the temptation to hoard what we have, to store up for a rainy day. We rationalize these actions as taking care of our family or preparing for the future. But this simply does not work! Unanticipated crises will always occur, things we have not or could not have prepared for. It is only by putting our trust in God and not in possessions that are with us here on earth that we can experience true abundance.

If we are to live out of abundance now and yet maintain some sense of material security in this physical world, then Christian community is of the utmost importance. In Jesus's parable in Luke 16 about the dishonest manager who, after losing his job, went to all his master's former clients and reduced their debt in order to gain their friendship, we see that we can "use worldly wealth to gain friends for yourselves, so that when it is gone, you will be welcomed into eternal dwellings" (Luke 16:9, NIV). The relationships we form with our fellow Christians are one of the few parts of our earthly lives that will carry over into the eternal. And while we are still on this side of eternity, the bonds formed in Christian community have a real impact on our earthly existence. Life together is *life together,* caring and bearing and sharing as if each joy and each struggle were our own. In addition to helping the downcast and downtrodden, we can use our wealth to build up the lives of fellow human beings. Chances are we will be living abundance.

REFLECTION QUESTION
Again, allow each member a few moments to answer this question.

✍ After everyone has had a chance to respond, the leader reads this paragraph.

What are some ways you can practice the ideology of abundance?

This concludes our look at living out God's abundance. In the next chapter we will turn our attention to another avenue of learning from Jesus—balancing Mary and Martha.

CLOSING PRAYER

The Lord is my shepherd, I shall not want.
>He makes me lie down in green pastures;
he leads me beside still waters;
>he restores my soul.
He leads me in right paths
>for his name's sake.

Even though I walk through the darkest valley,
  I fear no evil;
for you are with me;
  your rod and your staff—
  they comfort me.

You prepare a table before me
  in the presence of my enemies;
you anoint my head with oil;
  my cup overflows.
Surely goodness and mercy shall follow me
  all the days of my life,
and I shall dwell in the house of the LORD
  my whole life long. (PS 23)

TAKING IT FURTHER

✎ Allow some time for members to encourage one another to read the Devotional and Scripture Readings and do the exercise in the following chapter before the next meeting. Then invite the members to be silent for a few moments before leading them in reading the Closing Prayer aloud together.

✎ At the end of the Closing Prayer, the leader asks for a volunteer to lead the next meeting.

ADDITIONAL EXERCISE

Go through your closets, bookshelves, spare bedroom, or garage. With each item, ask yourself, "Could someone else make better use of this than I can?" Then collect those items for which the answer is yes to give to a local charitable organization. Set a goal for yourself—for instance, that you will give away two bags of clothes or twenty books—and try to meet or exceed it.

ADDITIONAL RESOURCES

Brueggemann, Walter. "Enough Is Enough." *The Other Side* (Nov/Dec 2001), 37, no. 6, 10–13.
Day, Dorothy. *The Long Loneliness: The Autobiography of Dorothy Day.* San Francisco: HarperSanFrancisco, 1980.
Foster, Richard J. *Freedom of Simplicity.* San Francisco: HarperSanFrancisco, 1986.
Myers, Ched. *The Biblical Vision of Sabbath Economics.* Washington, D.C.: Church of the Saviour, 2002.

ADDITIONAL REFLECTION QUESTIONS

Has there been a time when what you gave was multiplied into more than you expected?

How is sharing communion like sharing a meal? How is it different?

When sharing a meal with family and friends, do you always bless and give thanks for the food? Why or why not?

LEARNING FROM JESUS

BALANCING MARY AND MARTHA

KEY SCRIPTURE: Luke 10:38–42

DEVOTIONAL READING

EMILIE GRIFFIN, *The Reflective Executive*

From my first office in New York City, on the thirty-seventh floor of a Fifth Avenue tower, I could look down on St. Patrick's Cathedral. It looked like a child's plaything, a toy cathedral that I could lift and carry somewhere. Something about this troubled me. Cathedrals, I felt, should be looked up to. Later, when I visited England, I saw how cathedrals can dominate landscapes. Then I understood the new power balance of twentieth-century life. Lever House and the Seagram's Building, I concluded, are our new cathedrals. The Chrysler Building and the Empire State our statements of value. Dwarfing the little churches on Park Avenue and Wall Street, they have created a new ethos. These buildings are proclamations of power. Do we as executives need to leave these buildings in order to experience faith? Or is God with us in the Marketplace? . . .

God is here! He is actually present! It is not beneath him to dwell on the Staten Island ferry, heading for Lower Manhattan. He is willing to descend with us into the underground chambers of the subway, to be with us in discomfort, boredom, alienation. He accompanies us to the boardroom. He attends the year-end meeting. In the community formed by us, by colleagues, by purchasers, buyers and sellers, customers satisfied and unsatisfied, he is present, bearing our sorrows, acquainted with grief.

What a contrast to our common way of thinking: that business, which is by its very nature materialistic, somehow has to be spiritualized. The reality is otherwise. It is our mistake to think that we will somehow take business, which is unholy, and by some sacrifice or offering, make it holy. That tragic mistake is the crucial error we must expose. To correct this false notion we need not only action but contemplation. . . .

✍ It is helpful for everyone to read the Devotional and Scripture Readings and do the My Life with God Exercise before the meeting. Begin the meeting with silent prayer, then move directly to Reflecting on My Life with God below.

The reflective executive is one who walks by faith and thinks by metaphor; who sees in the terror and anxiety of the twentieth century a call to holiness, who understands daily experience as a call to conversion, who lives in dialogue with God, making intercession for others; who throws her own life into the breach when necessary; who manifests a concern for others; who takes into account, in business decisions, the intolerable sound of the word "trade-off" and at the same time the relentless necessity of compromise; who operates within the realm of the practical knowing that with God, all things are possible; who looks long, looks hard, looks prophetically and with vision at the improbable realignments that take place in society daily; who sets aside, to the extent possible, the biases, the *scotosis*, the distortions of ancient enmities and strife; and who longs for reconciliation, solidarity, sisterhood, brotherhood—perhaps for civility most of all.

The reflective executive is in short a hero and a saint, dressed in the ordinary garb of the marketplace. This executive is one who lives not only by getting things done but by getting the right things done because she lives in the sight of the Lord all days of her life. Her courage and her vision are unconquerable. She lives for her Master's counsel, and in his presence her heart is lifted up and consoled. She is anointed with the oil of gladness because she understands the generosity of the Lord's favor to her; and she is willing to walk through the canyons of cities built by commerce and weakened by double-dealing, to mend the broken statues, and to repair the shattered dreams.[1]

MY LIFE WITH GOD EXERCISE

In the Devotional Reading, Emilie Griffin writes about balancing an active life with a life of contemplation. Her work as a successful advertising executive was exhilarating. Yet in the maelstrom of frenetic activity, Emilie yearned for a place where her spirit could find rest during the most hectic days, maybe a location away from the noise and hustle and tension of New York City. In her search she spent time in prayer and contemplation at retreat centers. Emilie found that God was present, not only when she was actively seeking him in her leisure time, but also as she met with clients and supervised staff and created advertisements. God was with her in every facet of life—work, marriage, family, church, recreation, travel. That does not mean that she ceased setting aside times to come before God in simplicity and surrender. It does mean that instead of thinking that she could only be fully with God in some place other than the city or her job or with family, she found God was present in their midst.

Though we do not know how you experience God in your everyday life, we do know that most of us tend to err on the side of more action and less contemplation. So we ask you first to set aside at least fifteen minutes a day to come before the Lord. If you regularly set aside that much time or more each day, extend it by fifteen minutes. However, make sure that you do this in a *quiet* place. All telephones, radios, portable music players, computers, televisions—anything that emits noise made by humans—are to be put on hold or turned off. You should hear nothing, except natural sounds like birds singing or necessary noise like a furnace blower.

Next, try to quiet your heart and mind by asking God to take everything that is distracting you from coming fully into his presence. Getting rid of distractions is one of the hardest parts of contemplation, but with practice it is possible. Last, concentrate on God. It might help to read a favorite psalm or poem. Or focus on an icon or picture. Anything that helps keep your thoughts centered on God. If a distracting thought comes to mind, give it to God and ask him to bless it. Should this time become a burden or work instead of a joy, discontinue it for a few days, then try it again. At the end of each session, ask God to help you see his presence in everything you do, in everyone you meet, in every place you go during the coming day. And be sure to thank God for being with you.

We also suggest that you make a reservation for a twenty-four-hour retreat. This does not have to be done before the next gathering, but you should try to do it before the end of this study or soon thereafter. Try to find a center where they have a spiritual director on staff to help guide your retreat. If you don't feel comfortable asking for a spiritual director, Emilie Griffin has written a resource, *Wilderness Time*, to help in designing a one-day, three-day, or seven-day undirected retreat. Remember, the purpose of a retreat is to *be* in the presence of God, not to *do*.

What did you learn from your experience of contemplation?

REFLECTING ON MY LIFE WITH GOD
Allow each member a few moments to answer this question.

➤ **SCRIPTURE READING:** LUKE 10:38–42

Now as they went on their way, [Jesus] entered a certain village, where a woman named Martha welcomed him into her home. She had a sister named Mary, who sat at the Lord's feet and listened to what he was

After everyone has had a chance to respond to the question, ask a member to read this passage from Scripture.

saying. But Martha was distracted by her many tasks; so she came to him and asked, "Lord, do you not care that my sister has left me to do all the work by myself? Tell her then to help me." But the Lord answered her, "Martha, Martha, you are worried and distracted by many things; there is need of only one thing. Mary has chosen the better part, which will not be taken away from her."

REFLECTION QUESTION
Allow each person a few moments to respond to this question.

How do you think Mary felt when Martha told Jesus to have Mary help her? How do you think Martha felt when Jesus told her that what Mary was doing was all right?

▶▶ GETTING THE PICTURE

After a brief discussion, choose one person to read this section.

For those of us who have found ourselves in a situation similar to the one Martha was in—working hard to prepare a meal for a guest while other members of our family visit—Jesus's rebuke seems harsh. Others of us, however, see Martha as trying to manipulate Mary into doing what she wants her to and in the process putting Jesus in the middle. To help us better understand and interpret this passage, let's look a little more closely at how people in biblical times viewed hospitality.

Showing hospitality to a visitor was not optional in biblical times; cultural rules of hospitality were scrupulously observed. If you refused to be hospitable to a traveler, you would be in serious trouble with your neighbors, because each home was considered an extension of the community. When a guest was received into the home, the host—Luke writes that it was Martha—and the guest would have bowed to each other. They would have then kissed each other on the cheek, in the traditional greeting of the time. Next, Jesus would have removed his shoes, probably sandals, and Martha would have offered him water to wash his feet (see John 13:4–5), anointed his head with perfume or oil (Luke 7:46), and offered him a drink of water. But all of this was merely a prelude to the focal point of hospitality—the meal.

Although the text does not come right out and say it, it seems clear that Martha was busy preparing a meal for Jesus and other guests she may have had that evening. Then, as in much of the world today, the evening meal was the most important aspect of showing hospitality. The typical evening meal served to guests consisted of meat, seasonal vegetables and fruit, bread, and either milk, water, or wine. Some fruits like figs were dried and served in cakes. The cooked food was prepared over a fire in an open hearth either in pottery containers or on spits. Since there was no refrigeration, preparing the evening meal was no small task. Every day Martha would have gone to the market, cleaned and cooked the food, set service around a low table, and served the food. The text doesn't make it clear, but it is possible that all the disciples were at Martha's house with Jesus. Having that many guests would have increased the work, and possibly explains why Martha felt like she needed help.

▶▶▶ GOING DEEPER

In the context of these cultural expectations about hospitality, we can understand Martha's request a little better. She was trying to abide by the rules of hospitality and thought Mary should be helping her. But Martha had forgotten that the reason for the customs of hospitality was to make visitors feel welcome and comfortable, to show them honor and respect. Instead Martha let her focus shift from Jesus to her domestic duties, from a personal relationship to earthly concerns. Martha had welcomed Jesus into her house, then got so busy with the details of being a good hostess that she apparently forgot why she had invited him to her home in the first place. Of course, we don't know exactly why she invited him to her home. Perhaps it was to show off her house and prove to Jesus what a great hostess she was. Or because she knew that he and Lazarus, her brother, were good friends. But perhaps it was because she wanted to know more about the with-God life and the kingdom Jesus was proclaiming, and while Martha was distracted by her work, Mary was learning about the kingdom by listening to Jesus's teachings.

Have another member read this section.

Notice the way Jesus corrects Martha's assumption that Mary should be assisting her. In saying Martha's name not once but twice when he responds to her, Jesus shows deep affection for Martha. It is much like we say the names of our children when they ask for something or want to do something that is not for their own good: "Micah, Micah, you don't know what you are asking for." You can almost hear the tenderness and compassion in Jesus's response. It reminds us that when we ask Jesus in our prayers to do things for us that aren't in our best interests, he will lovingly say no and direct us to a better way.

The story of Mary and Martha prompts us to keep in mind that the Holy Spirit gives a variety of gifts: teaching, prophecy, hospitality, speaking in tongues. Martha seems to have had the gifts of hospitality and action; Mary seems to have had the gifts of learning and contemplation. Each of us has different gifts and is called to serve God and those around us in different ways (1 Pet 4:10). It's not up to us to try to shoehorn others into serving the same way we do. Just because we are called to lead a mission trip doesn't mean that someone else is suited for the same ministry; perhaps welcoming new members is that person's best ministry. Sometimes our fellow Christians are serving in ways that are not evident to us, at times even in ways that we don't even think of as service. We should joyfully carry out the service we feel called to, but we should not expect everyone to join us in that particular area of kingdom work.

The Scripture also teaches us that balance is required in the spiritual life. Although we need to caution ourselves against trying to push others into activities and attitudes for which they may not be suited, at the same time we need to challenge ourselves to develop those spiritual muscles that are weak. Those of us who take part in numerous service and mission activities still need silent time alone with God, just as those of us who excel at study and contemplative prayer need to engage positively with the world around us. There are times when, like Martha, we should be actively serving others. There are other times when we should be like Mary, sitting at the feet of Jesus. In their extremes both frantic activity and quiet contemplation are destructive. The extreme activist can become exhausted and resentful of people who are not helping or who seem not to care about the projects he or she feels are important. Many times the extreme contemplative disengages from the world and from projects that are vital to spreading the message of God's love and kingdom. As Parker J. Palmer wrote in *The Active Life,* "Contemplation and action ought not to be at war with one another, and as long as they are, we will be at war with ourselves."[2] To be spiritually healthy, we must find a balance between action and contemplation, between doing and being—a balance that fits us where we are in learning from Jesus how to be his disciple.

REFLECTION QUESTION
Allow each person a few moments to respond.

Evaluate your own spiritual balance. Do you lean more toward the contemplative or the active? Where are you doing well and where do you need improvement?

LEARNING FROM JESUS

Brother Lawrence, a seventeenth-century French monk, found that the best way to marry the contemplative and active aspects of the Christian life was to continually practice the presence of God. Brother Lawrence worked mostly in the kitchen during his years at the monastery, yet he was recognized then and now as a great man of spirituality. In the midst of his culinary adventures he achieved just what Emilie Griffin wrote about in the Devotional Reading—the knowledge that God was with him during all his daily duties. After years of trying to be constantly aware of the presence of God, Brother Lawrence found himself able to bask in God's presence virtually all the time. All distinctions between prayer and work or recreational life fell away. As he wrote, "The most excellent method I have found of going to God is that of doing common business without any view to pleasing men, and as far as I am capable, doing it purely for the love of God. It is a great delusion to think that the time of prayer ought to be different from other times. We are strictly obliged to adhere to God in the time of action, just as we are to adhere to prayer during the season of prayer. My prayers are nothing more than a sense of the presence of God. My soul is simply insensible, at that time, to anything but divine love. When the appointed time of prayer has passed, I find no difference because I still continue with God, praising and blessing him with all my might, so that I might pass my life in continual joy."[3]

For those of us who may find the idea of continuous prayer daunting, Brother Lawrence offered some practical advice for starting out: "The Lord does not really lay any great burden on us. He only wants you to recall Him to mind as often as possible, to pour out your adoration on Him, to pray for His grace. Offer Him your sorrows. Return from time to time to Him, and quietly, purely thank Him for the benefit He has given you in knowing Him. Thank Him, too, for the benefit He pours out on you even in the midst of your troubles.... Lift your heart to the Lord at every meal, even when you have company.... Begin now to accustom yourself, little by little, to worshipping Him. Ask Him for grace. Offer Him your whole heart. Over and again, in the midst of business, every moment if you can, just offer Him your heart. (This can be done without a single utterance escaping you. Or, you can express yourself quietly, yet audibly, by whispering your love to Him.) Do not get weighted down with a lot of rules, or forms, or ways; act with faith—just come."[4]

✍ Choose one member to read this section.

✍ Have another person read this section.

Brother Lawrence teaches us that the best way to find balance in our spiritual lives is to keep our attention focused on Jesus. As Jesus's response to Martha's demand reminds us, it is all too easy to get distracted from keeping our focus on him. Martha's mistake was forgetting that hospitality was ultimately about the guest. Mary, on the other hand, had her attention focused right where it should be: on Jesus. "There is need of only one thing," Jesus told Martha, and this is a lesson we should remember. Ultimately, all things in our lives should flow from one thing: our relationship with Jesus.

And our relationship with Jesus permeates all of our life. Thus, as Emilie Griffin, Brother Lawrence, and the Scripture passage all teach us, it is unhelpful to make a false distinction between the active and the contemplative life. The reality is that if we accustom ourselves to searching for God's presence, we realize that he is just as present with us in a business meeting or class as he is when we are praying. As *The Renovaré Spiritual Formation Bible* says, "Our discipleship is incarnational at all times, not just in religious moments. Inner Christlikeness does not just include our religious rituals and moral character. These are fundamental, to be sure, but real inner Christlikeness makes every act of family, business, and community a time of learning how to live our life as Jesus would live it. Remember, for all but the last few years Jesus's life was in domestic contexts much like our own. Under his tutelage we learn how to make heavenly friends by managing, under God, 'mammon.' Being faithful in the 'very little' trains us for being faithful 'in much,' in 'the true riches' that God possesses and will place in our charge when he knows we are ready (Luke 16:9–12)."[5]

REFLECTION QUESTION
Again, allow each member a few moments to answer this question.

In what areas of your life do you have the most trouble sensing God—work, family, recreation, hobbies? What do you think prevents you from sensing God's presence in these areas? How might you be able to focus more on God at these times?

✍ After everyone has had a chance to respond, the leader reads this paragraph.

This concludes our look at balancing Mary and Martha. In the next chapter we will turn our attention to another avenue of learning from Jesus—bearing the cross.

CLOSING PRAYER

The LORD is my shepherd, I shall not want.
　　He makes me lie down in green pastures;
he leads me beside still waters;
　　he restores my soul.
He leads me in right paths
　　for his name's sake.

Even though I walk through the darkest valley,
　　I fear no evil;
for you are with me;
　　your rod and your staff—
　　they comfort me.

You prepare a table before me
　　in the presence of my enemies;
you anoint my head with oil;
　　my cup overflows.
Surely goodness and mercy shall follow me
　　all the days of my life,
and I shall dwell in the house of the LORD
　　my whole life long. (PS 23)

Allow some time for members to encourage one another to read Devotional and Scripture Readings and do the exercise in the following chapter before the next meeting. Then invite the members to be silent for a few moments before leading them in reading the Closing Prayer aloud together.

At the end of the Closing Prayer, the leader asks for a volunteer to lead the next meeting.

TAKING IT FURTHER

Balance is essential to the spiritual life. The need for balance is a driving force behind RENOVARÉ. RENOVARÉ identifies six essential dimensions, or streams, of the spiritual life—Contemplative: The Prayer-Filled Life; Holiness: The Virtuous Life; Charismatic: The Spirit-Empowered Life; Social Justice: The Compassionate Life; Evangelical: The Word-Centered Life; and Incarnational: The Sacramental Life. To learn more about these traditions of Christian faith and practice, consult the RENOVARÉ Web site at www.renovare.org, or read *Streams of Living Water* by Richard J. Foster.

ADDITIONAL EXERCISE

ADDITIONAL RESOURCES

Brother Lawrence and Frank Laubach. *Practicing His Presence.*
　　Jacksonville, FL: Seedsowers/Christian Books, 1988.
Foster, Richard J. *Streams of Living Water.* San Francisco:
　　HarperSanFrancisco, 1998.
Griffin, Emilie. *The Reflective Executive.* New York: Crossroad, 1993.

Griffin, Emilie. *Wilderness Time*. San Francisco: HarperSanFrancisco, 1997.

Palmer, Parker J. *The Active Life*. San Francisco: Jossey-Bass, 1990.

What are your main spiritual gifts?

In what areas do you need to strengthen yourself spiritually?

How do our culture's standards of hospitality differ from those of Jesus's culture? How can you better practice Christian hospitality?

BEARING
THE CROSS

11

KEY SCRIPTURE: Matthew 10:34–39

DEVOTIONAL READING

FRANÇOIS FÉNELON, *Talking with God*

We must carry the cross as a treasure. It is through the cross that we are made worthy of God and conformed to the likeness of his Son. Crosses are a part of our daily bread. God regulates the measure of them according to our real wants, which he knows, and of which we are ignorant. Let him do as he wills, and let us resign ourselves into his hands.

Be a child of divine providence. Leave it to your relatives and friends to reason about things. Do not think about the future from afar. The manna was corrupted when, out of prudent foresight, they wished to provide sufficient supply for more than one day. Do not say, What shall we do tomorrow? "Tomorrow will worry about itself" [St. Matthew 6:34 (NIV)]. Confine yourself today to your present needs. God will give you each day the help that is proportioned to that day. "Those who seek the Lord lack no good thing" [Psalm 34:10 (NIV)]. Providence would do miracles for us, but we hinder these miracles by trying to anticipate them. We make for ourselves, by our restless industry, a providence as defective as the providence of God would be certain.

Be faithful and docile. By an infinite distrust of yourself make your weaknesses profitable, and by a childlike pliability allow yourself to be corrected. Humility will be your strength, even in the midst of weakness.

I do not doubt that our Lord will always treat you as one of his friends; that is to say, he will send you crosses, sufferings, humiliations. These ways and means, which God makes use of to draw souls to himself, do this work so much better and more quickly than the creature's own efforts; for the very fact of its being God's action alone is destructive

It is helpful for everyone to read the Devotional and Scripture Readings and do the My Life with God Exercise before the meeting. Begin the meeting with silent prayer, then move directly to Reflecting on My Life with God below.

to self-love and tears up the roots which we cannot even discover without great difficulty. But God, who knows all the secret lurking places of self-love, proceeds forthwith to attack it in its stronghold, and upon its own ground.

If we were strong enough and faithful enough to trust ourselves entirely to God, and to follow him simply wherever he wished to lead us, we should have no need of great application of mind to labour in the work of our perfection. But because we are so weak in faith that we wish to know where we are going, without trusting to God, our way becomes much longer, and spoils our spiritual affairs.

Abandon yourself as much as you can to God, until your last breath, and he will never forsake you.[1]

MY LIFE WITH GOD EXERCISE

Nothing showcases our humanity more than our inability to submit—to loved ones, to authorities, to God. Our cross is not made of wood; our cross is made of flesh. It is our self wrapped in flesh. With arms outstretched it may be the same shape as Jesus's wooden cross, but our embodied self has the ability to ignore and disregard, resist and disobey. No one has to teach a child to ignore his or her parents' wishes. Children seem to have a built-in switch that turns off their hearing the moment a parent asks them to do something. Nor does anyone have to teach a child to say no. It is among the first words in most toddlers' vocabulary. And they know what it means. They know that if they say *no* forcefully and loudly enough, many times they will get their own way. As much as we hate to admit it, seeking to get our own way is part and parcel of our self-centered human nature.

This condition of selfishness can only be cured by submitting to the will of others or to what is best for others. In that submitting we die to self. We die to our self-centeredness. We die to always wanting our own way. We die to wishing for a different life or job. We die to always blaming others for our failures. The biblical writers knew that only submission would cure the disease of narcissism, that is, excessive self-admiration and self-reflection. The apostle Paul wrote, "Children, obey your parents. . . . Slaves, obey your earthly masters" (Eph 6:1, 5). Christians are advised to "be subject to one another" (Eph 5:21), to "obey your leaders and submit to them, for they are keeping watch over your souls and will give an account" (Heb 13:17a), and to "submit yourselves therefore to God" (James 4:7a). All admonish us to break the bucking bronco of self-centeredness in the arenas of our life.

To this clamor François Fénelon adds his voice: "Carry the cross as a treasure," "Let us resign ourselves into [God's] hands," "Be a child of divine providence," "Confine yourself today to your present needs," "Be faithful and docile," "Abandon yourself as much as you can to God." However, neither Fénelon nor the biblical writers suggest specific things we can do to solve this difficult problem, other than to persevere through the "crosses, sufferings, and humiliations" God sends our way. We hear only advice that seems divorced from practice.

In this exercise we will work to be more intentional about the discipline of submission. List by name all the authorities in your life: work supervisor, church leadership, government (local, state, and federal), and any others you can think of. Include relationships—your spouse, child, parent, fellow Christians. Leave space around the items to make notes. After the list is complete, write in large letters across the page: "GOD." During the coming days, pay attention to those authorities and the specific ways in which you are asked or required to submit to them. Note them on your list. For example, you might write down something your supervisor tells you to do and your reaction to that request. Or note that you broke a law by going faster than the speed limit on your way to work. If there is anything you disagree with or chafe under, take that issue to God and ask him to help you submit to that person's or entity's authority. (Always bear in mind that there are times when we shouldn't submit to the authority of a person or entity—times when our safety or well-being is at stake or someone is taking inappropriate advantage of us; ask God to help you discern these times.)

Specifically watch for times when you fail to submit to the counsel of God given through the written Word, the Bible; the incarnate Word, Jesus Christ; or the indwelling Word, the Holy Spirit. It is only as we become aware of when our spirits rebel and our self-will asserts itself that we are able to bring our will under control, much like we control a horse with a bit. The bit we use is not made of steel; God gives us the means to help take charge of our self-will—the disciplines of submission and prayer. (For a more complete discussion of the Spiritual Disciplines, see either "The With-God Life" in this guide or *The Renovaré Spiritual Formation Bible* [San Francisco: HarperSanFrancisco, 2005], pp. xxv–xxxvi.)

REFLECTING ON MY
LIFE WITH GOD
Allow each member a few
moments to answer this
question.

What were some of the times you found yourself struggling to submit? How did this exercise make you feel about submission?

➤ SCRIPTURE READING: MATTHEW 10:34–39

↷ After everyone has
had a chance to respond
to the question, ask a
member to read this pas-
sage from Scripture.

[Jesus said,] "Do not think that I have come to bring peace to the earth; I have not come to bring peace, but a sword.

> For I have come to set a man against his father,
> and a daughter against her mother,
> and a daughter-in-law against her mother-in-law;
> and one's foes will be members of one's own household.

Whoever loves father or mother more than me is not worthy of me; and whoever loves son or daughter more than me is not worthy of me; and whoever does not take up the cross and follow me is not worthy of me. Those who find their life will lose it, and those who lose their life for my sake will find it."

REFLECTION QUESTION
Allow each person a few
moments to respond to
this question.

What is your initial reaction to this passage? What does it mean to you to take up your cross and follow Jesus?

➤➤ GETTING THE PICTURE

↷ After a brief discus-
sion, choose one person
to read this section.

Our Scripture Reading comes toward the end of a teaching that Jesus gives his twelve disciples as they prepare to go on a healing mission "to the lost sheep of the house of Israel" (Matt 10:6). During the trip they are to proclaim that the kingdom of God has come and is available to all. In addition, he gives them authority to "cure the sick, raise the dead, cleanse the lepers, cast out demons" (v 8). Jesus gives specific instructions about what disciples are to take with them, where they are to stay, and how they are to treat people who do not welcome them. At the end of the traveling instructions, he speaks frankly about what the disciples may face on their trip, including floggings, interrogations, and hatred, because he knows their message will turn people against them, even relatives against each other. They are not to worry about what they will say before the councils when brought up on charges, because the Holy

Spirit will speak through them, and he directs that they should flee a town when they are persecuted. Jesus tells the disciples they are not to fear those who can kill their bodies; they are to fear God, "who can destroy both soul and body in hell" (vv 26–31). While telling the disciples how precious they are, he tells them that whoever "acknowledges me before others, I also will acknowledge before my Father in heaven; but whoever denies me before others, I also will deny before my Father in heaven" (vv 32–33).

These verses are hard to understand if we think that Jesus came only to bring God's love into the world. In order to think more clearly about the Scripture Reading, read Eugene Peterson's translation of Matthew 10:34–39 in *The Message:*

> "Don't think I've come to make life cozy. I've come to cut—make a sharp knife-cut between son and father, daughter and mother, bride and mother-in-law—cut through these cozy domestic arrangements and free you for God. Well-meaning family members can be your worst enemies. If you prefer father or mother over me, you don't deserve me. If you prefer son or daughter over me, you don't deserve me.
>
> "If you don't go all the way with me, through thick and thin, you don't deserve me. If your first concern is to look after yourself, you'll never find yourself. But if you forget about yourself and look to me, you'll find both yourself and me."[2]

Jesus could not have been more frank with the disciples. He has called them and taught them; now it is time to put that teaching into practice. However, they are not going to have it easy. They are going to face opposition and hostility even from their own family members. Not only that—later Jesus tells them that they will have to deny themselves if they want to be his disciples: "If any want to become my followers, let them deny themselves and take up their cross and follow me. For those who want to save their life will lose it, and those who lose their life for my sake will find it. For what will it profit them if they gain the whole world but forfeit their life? Or what will they give in return for their life?" (Matt 16:24–26).

For the twelve going out on their first missionary trip, being a disciple of Jesus in the kingdom of God is self-shifting business. No longer can they focus their attention on themselves. They are to die to their self-interest and self-absorption. Their reward for losing their life in Jesus Christ? A seeming oxymoron: they will gain their life (Matt 16:25).

✐ Have another member read this section.

Bearing the cross is intimately linked to becoming a disciple of Jesus, and one of a disciple's most important traits is teachability—having a heart open to the things of God. From what we can glean from the biblical record, Jesus was with the first disciples 24/7. Those who chose to be disciples of Jesus learned how to be disciples *from* Jesus. They were his apprentices in learning to heal the sick, communicate the good news, restore sight to the blind, and make manifest the ever-present kingdom of God.

From the time Jesus took to prepare the disciples for this journey, we learn that all disciples must be prepared before they can teach others how to be a disciple. As in any vocation or profession, some learn faster than others, but we all learn how to be a disciple from another disciple. Becoming a disciple of Jesus Christ does not happen automatically when we put our trust in him; it takes time and training—time and training that many of us may not be willing to undergo once we consider what it will cost (Luke 14:25–33).

A disciple of Jesus must be willing to die to self and face the challenges inherent in this calling. As we said, putting aside our own self-interest takes much prayer and travail. It is not easy to train our spirits to submit to the authority of those we are around daily. Likewise, it is hard to submit to the authority of the Father, Son, and Holy Spirit. Jesus taught in a parable that there will be some people who enthusiastically enter into the kingdom of God but fall away once it is fully clear what it means to be a disciple (Mark 4:1–9). Today, as it was for the original disciples, being a disciple of Christ is not for the hesitant; it is for those committed to living out the fullness of God's vision and presence, with ever-increasing disregard for what it costs personally. We can be assured, though, that after we make the leap from looking out only for ourselves to putting the interests of Christ and his kingdom first, we will be ready to undergo whatever comes our way for the sake of furthering that kingdom.

As we gain a vision of life from Jesus Christ and put it into practice as best we can, we realize there is both a "cost of discipleship," as Dietrich Bonhoeffer puts it, and a "cost of nondiscipleship," as Dallas Willard makes clear. The "cost of discipleship" relates to life as we know it. Each day we have priorities, needs, wants, and a sense of how our day-to-day comings and goings should be ordered and attained if life is to be meaningful and full-bodied. Submitting our lives to Jesus, taking up our crosses and following him, puts our present lifestyle at risk. As we submit our lives to Jesus Christ, our lives change. The insecurity and instability engendered by our change in priorities and way of living are the costs of discipleship.

The "cost of nondiscipleship," on the other hand, is the life we sacrifice if we pursue our self-centered, narcissistic ways. As Dallas Willard puts it, "The cost of nondiscipleship is far greater—even when this [earthly] life alone is considered—than the price paid to walk with Jesus. Nondiscipleship costs abiding peace, a life penetrated throughout by love, faith that sees everything in the light of God's overriding governance for good, hopefulness that stands firm in the most discouraging of circumstances, power to do what is right and withstand the forces of evil. In short, it costs exactly that abundance of life Jesus said he came to bring (John 10:10)."[3] The cost of nondiscipleship is the cost of not living our lives from Jesus, choosing this life of worldly insecurity instead of living the life of eternal security that begins the moment we submit ourselves to the life Jesus Christ has waiting for us. Nondiscipleship costs us a life of peace, security, confidence, and partnering with Jesus to nurture the individual and communal possibilities that only God can bring about. Nondiscipleship costs us "the life that really is life" (1 Tim 6:19b).

Last, and perhaps the most important, disciples of Jesus never take their focus off him. He is their teacher; he gives them the power for what they do; he is at the center of what they do. As Fénelon wrote, "Abandon yourself as much as you can to God." In that abandonment to God we abandon our own self-interest and focus on Jesus Christ. We take up the fleshly cross and follow Jesus Christ wherever he leads, because "it is through the cross that we are made worthy of God and conformed to the likeness of his Son."[4]

How did the perceived costs of discipleship affect your decision to follow Christ? What would have been some of the costs of nondiscipleship if you had not decided to learn how to live from Jesus?

REFLECTION QUESTION
Allow each person a few moments to respond.

▶▶▶▶ POINTING TO GOD

Throughout history, following Jesus's command to take up our crosses and follow him has led Christians on unexpected paths. There could

✍ Choose one member to read this section.

hardly be a better example than Lilias Trotter, a British woman born into the upper class of Victorian England, who gave up her comfortable life and burgeoning career as an artist to serve God as a missionary in North Africa.

Even as a young girl, Trotter was a devout Christian, but when she was in her twenties influential encounters with Robert Pearsall Smith, Hannah Whitall Smith, and Dwight Moody helped Lilias focus her faith on works of service. She taught Sunday school and volunteered frequently in support of mission work. Meanwhile, Lilias enjoyed sketching and painting watercolor landscapes of the beautiful locations she and her family visited on their many travels abroad.

When Lilias and her mother took a long holiday in Venice, they met John Ruskin, the noted British art critic, and Mrs. Trotter showed him Lilias's artwork. Ruskin, who had been convinced that "women could not paint or draw," was dazzled. He took it upon himself to teach technique to Lilias, who had very little training in art. The two developed a lifelong friendship, and a few years later, Ruskin, even more convinced of her potential, urged twenty-six-year-old Lilias to devote herself to art. This challenge provoked a crisis in faith for Lilias, who felt that she must now choose between a life dedicated to art and a life dedicated to the service of God. She struggled with the decision and finally made the only choice she could: "I see as clear as daylight now, I cannot give myself to painting in the way that he means and continue still to 'seek first the Kingdom of God and His Righteousness.'"[5]

Trotter realized that her decision would seem harsh and perhaps unnecessary to some. In *Parables of the Cross,* she wrote about her decision: "Does all this seem hard? Does any soul, young in physical or in spiritual life, shrink back and say, 'I would rather keep in the springtime. I do not want to reach unto the things that are before if it means all this pain.' To such comes the Master's voice, 'Fear none of these things which Thou shalt suffer.'"[6]

Lilias did not entirely give up her painting, but it did cause her lifelong pain to know that she might have given up a tremendously successful career as a painter and the acclaim that would have accompanied it. Still, she was clear that she had given up something good for something better—submission to Christ. Lilias embarked upon a remarkable forty-year career as a missionary to Algeria, where she founded the Algiers Mission Band, an evangelical interdenominational ministry that grew from just three women to thirty workers and in 1964 merged with the North African Mission. Her writings include a colloquial Arabic translation of the New Testament, *Parables of the Cross, The Master of the Impossible, Between the Desert and the Sea,* and *The Way of the Sevenfold Secret.*

>>>>> **GOING FORWARD**

Bearing the cross and entering the kingdom of God is a joyful prospect, but it is also a daunting one. Not only does Jesus not promise worldly wealth and happiness, but he guarantees that the journey of discipleship will not be easy. We can all expect our with-God life journey to be full of crosses. As Dietrich Bonhoeffer wrote in *The Cost of Discipleship,* "When Christ calls us he bids us come and die."[7]

We are to die, to die so that Christ can give us life—a difficult concept that the example of Lilias Trotter helps us understand. She knew that to give herself fully to her desire to be a painter was not what was asked of her as a follower of Christ. Her ultimate path was not the one she would have chosen if she had listened to her instincts and the world around her. Truly she knew what it was to die to self and to live fully in Christ. Dying to self is what happens when we turn our attention away from the selfish demands and desires of our own bodies and egos and find that Jesus Christ calls us instead to see to the spiritual and physical needs of others. The astonishing thing, as Lilias Trotter discovered, is that it is in working for the good of others in Jesus's name that we find true fulfillment. In the end we realize that our discipleship to Jesus leads us away from a life lived for ourselves and toward a life lived for others. As Thomas Aquinas said, "Christ did not lay down his life for us as enemies so that we should remain enemies, but so that he could make us friends."[8]

What in your life is challenging your commitment to be a disciple of Jesus Christ?

This concludes our look at bearing the cross. In the next chapter we will turn our attention to another avenue of learning from Jesus—abiding in Christ.

> Have another person read this section.

REFLECTION QUESTION
Again, allow each member a few moments to answer this question.

> After everyone has had a chance to respond, the leader reads this paragraph.

Allow some time for members to encourage one another to read the Devotional and Scripture Readings and do the exercise in the following chapter before the next meeting. Then invite the members to be silent for a few moments before leading them in reading the Closing Prayer aloud together.

At the end of the Closing Prayer, the leader asks for a volunteer to lead the next meeting.

CLOSING PRAYER

The LORD is my shepherd, I shall not want.
    He makes me lie down in green pastures;
he leads me beside still waters;
    he restores my soul.
He leads me in right paths
    for his name's sake.

Even though I walk through the darkest valley,
    I fear no evil;
for you are with me;
      your rod and your staff—
    they comfort me.

You prepare a table before me
    in the presence of my enemies;
you anoint my head with oil;
    my cup overflows.
Surely goodness and mercy shall follow me
    all the days of my life,
and I shall dwell in the house of the LORD
    my whole life long. (PS 23)

TAKING IT FURTHER

ADDITIONAL EXERCISE

We saw in this chapter that one way to die to self is to focus on service to other people, putting their needs before our own. Look into service opportunities within your church and community—volunteering at a soup kitchen or shelter, delivering meals to the ill and elderly, mentoring a boy or girl—and spend some time in prayer, seeking to discern whether one of these opportunities is an appropriate and timely commitment for you.

ADDITIONAL RESOURCES

Fénelon, François. *Talking with God.* Translated by Hal M. Helms. Brewster, MA: Paraclete, 1997.

Rockness, Miriam Huffman. *A Passion for the Impossible: The Life of Lilias Trotter.* Grand Rapids, MI: Discovery House, 2003.

Trotter, I. Lilias. *Parables of the Cross.* Marshall Brothers, 1890.

What are some ways that well-meaning family members can get in the way of our discipleship? Is this an issue in your life? Explain.

Other than submission, how can we work to die to self?

Have you ever had to make a sacrifice like Lilias Trotter's, in order to better follow Christ? If so, how?

12

ABIDING IN CHRIST

KEY SCRIPTURE: John 15:1–11

DEVOTIONAL READING

THOMAS R. KELLY, *A Testament of Devotion*

Deep within us all there is an amazing inner sanctuary of the soul, a holy place, a Divine Center, a speaking Voice, to which we may continuously return. Eternity is at our hearts, pressing upon our time-torn lives, warming us with intimations of an astounding destiny, calling us home unto Itself. Yielding to these persuasions, gladly committing ourselves in body and soul, utterly and completely, to the Light Within, is the beginning of true life. It is a dynamic center, a creative Life that presses to birth within us. It is a Light Within which illumines the face of God and casts new shadows and new glories upon the face of men. It is a seed stirring to life if we do not choke it. It is the Shekinah of the soul, the Presence in the midst. Here is the Slumbering Christ, stirring to be awakened, to become the soul we clothe in earthly form and action. And He is within us all.

You who read these words already know this inner Life and Light. For by this very Light within you, is your recognition given. In this humanistic age we suppose man is the initiator and God is the responder. But the Living Christ within us is the initiator and we are the responders. God the Lover, the accuser, the revealer of light and darkness presses within us. "Behold I stand at the door and knock." And all our apparent initiative is already a response, a testimonial to His secret presence and working within us.

The basic response of the soul to the Light is internal adoration and joy, thanksgiving and worship, self-surrender and listening. The secret places of the heart cease to be our noisy workshop. They become

It is helpful for everyone to read the Devotional and Scripture Readings and do the My Life with God Exercise before the meeting. Begin the meeting with silent prayer, then move directly to Reflecting on My Life with God below.

a holy sanctuary of adoration and of self-oblation, where we are kept in perfect peace, if our minds be stayed on Him who has found us in the inward springs of our life. And in brief intervals of overpowering visitation we are able to carry the sanctuary frame of mind out into the world, into its turmoil and its fitfulness, and in a hyperaesthesia of the soul, we see all mankind tinged with deeper shadows, and touched with Galilean glories. Powerfully are the springs of our will moved to an abandon of singing love toward God; powerfully are we moved to a new and overcoming love toward time-blinded men and all creation. In this Center of Creation all things are ours, and we are Christ's and Christ is God's. We are owned men, ready to run and not be weary and to walk and not faint. . . .

How then, shall we lay hold of that Life and Power, and live the life of prayer without ceasing? By quiet, persistent practice in turning of all our being, day and night, in prayer and inward worship and surrender, toward Him who calls in the deeps of our souls. Mental habits of inward orientation must be established. An inner, secret turning to God can be made fairly steady, after weeks and months and years of practice and lapses and failures and returns. It is as simple an art as Brother Lawrence found it, but it may be long before we achieve any steadiness in the process. Begin now as you read these words, as you sit in your chair, to offer your whole selves, utterly and in joyful abandon, in quiet, glad surrender to Him who is within. In secret ejaculations of praise, turn in humble wonder to the Light, faint though it may be. Keep contact with the outer world of sense and meanings. Here is no discipline in absent-mindedness. Walk and talk and work and laugh with your friends. But behind the scenes, keep up the life of simple prayer and inward worship. Keep it up throughout the day. Let inward prayer be your last act before you fall asleep and the first act when you awake. And in time you will find, as did Brother Lawrence, that "those who have the gale of the Holy Spirit go forward even in sleep."[1]

MY LIFE WITH GOD EXERCISE

In the Devotional Reading, Thomas Kelly eloquently explains what it means to abide in Christ. To abide in Christ is to realize he is our resting place, our true home. It is an inward knowledge of the presence of God that initiates all the good in our lives. It is the indwelling of Christ in us. Christ is in us and we in him; abiding in Christ also means reaching the point where we are constantly aware of that indwelling, in communion with Christ. Kelly discusses the perfect peace we can find "if our minds be stayed on Him." This seems to most of us a difficult task, but Kelly and others, such as Brother Lawrence, Frank Laubach, and Teresa of Avila, attest to the fact that it is indeed possible. This week, seek to do just what Kelly describes: return as often as you can to that internal sanctuary, that place where Christ abides in you and you in him. Follow Kelly's advice: offer prayer as you are preparing to sleep and as soon as you awake. Do not ignore the outer world but instead seek to be in praise and worship of God even as you engage with it. Kelly warns that when we first attempt to keep our minds "stayed on God," we will focus alternately on the things around us and the Light of Christ within. He urges that we not be discouraged in those inevitable moments in which we realize that a long period of time has passed since we have turned our attention inward, but to "breathe a silent prayer for forgiveness and begin again, just where you are. Offer *this* broken worship up to Him and say: 'This is what I am except Thou aid me.'"[2] It may help to write down your thoughts and to note the places and times where you need to work harder to turn your attention inward to God. Keeping something with you, such as a small, smooth stone in your pocket or a bracelet around your wrist, may also help remind you of your constant communion with God.

At the end of the week assess your progress in living in constant awareness of and communion with God. Think of the different areas of your life—your relationship with a spouse, with children, with other family members, with friends, your small group Bible study, church, job, neighborhood, service club, social organizations, the community at large. When, where, and with whom were you best able to succeed, and when did you find it most difficult? Many of us, for example, will probably admit to having a difficult time maintaining our sense of communication with God when we are driving in heavy traffic.

Now pray over what you discover, thanking God for allowing you to abide in him at all times and asking him to help you become even more aware of the need to abide in him, to know that "our life is the life of Christ." Feel free to ask God to help you overcome a lack of trust in him, to fill you with the Holy Spirit, and to help in any other area that may be hindering your ability to abide in Christ and let Christ abide in you. It would be good to pray repeatedly about this as you continue to seek this constant knowledge of and communion with Christ.

REFLECTING ON MY LIFE WITH GOD
Allow each member a few moments to answer this question.

After doing the exercise, how well do you feel you are abiding in Christ and letting Christ abide in you?

✍ After everyone has had a chance to respond to the question, ask a member to read this passage from Scripture.

➤ SCRIPTURE READING: JOHN 15:1–11

"I am the true vine, and my Father is the vinegrower. He removes every branch in me that bears no fruit. Every branch that bears fruit he prunes to make it bear more fruit. You have already been cleansed by the word that I have spoken to you. Abide in me as I abide in you. Just as the branch cannot bear fruit by itself unless it abides in the vine, neither can you unless you abide in me. I am the vine, you are the branches. Those who abide in me and I in them bear much fruit, because apart from me you can do nothing. Whoever does not abide in me is thrown away like a branch and withers; such branches are gathered, thrown into the fire, and burned. If you abide in me, and my words abide in you, ask for whatever you wish, and it will be done for you. My Father is glorified by this, that you bear much fruit and become my disciples. As the Father has loved me, so I have loved you; abide in my love. If you keep my commandments, you will abide in my love, just as I have kept my Father's commandments and abide in his love. I have said these things to you so that my joy may be in you, and that your joy may be complete."

What does the image of Christ as the vine and you as a branch mean to you?

REFLECTION QUESTION
Allow each person a few moments to respond to this question.

➤➤ GETTING THE PICTURE

✍ After a brief discussion, choose one person to read this section.

The Scripture Reading is part of Jesus's last teachings to the disciples before his death. These teachings, which he gives them in the guest room during the Passover meal and as they are leaving Jerusalem, are recorded only in the gospel of John, chapters 13–17. Just before the Scripture Reading, Jesus foretells his betrayal, gives the disciples a new commandment, predicts Peter's denial, tells them that he is the way to the Father, and promises that the Holy Spirit will be with them. In the Reading he uses the metaphor of a grapevine and its fruit to teach the disciples how to live a fruitful life.

To understand the metaphor, it is helpful to know more about how grapevines are raised and pruned. Grapes are planted between two posts between which two strands of smooth trellis wire have been secured and stretched. In the most common configuration, a new vine is trained so that the trunk goes straight up and four branches, or canes, grow out at right angles, two on each side, supported by the wires. The vine and its branches require a great deal of care. They must be watered and pruned at the right time. In early spring, after the vine starts producing, the small shoots and excess buds are trimmed off the one-year-old growth and disposed of. Only the buds that will bear fruit are left to receive the life-giving sap from the vine. A branch that receives no sap will dry up, wither, and die.

Occasionally new grafts are attached to the vine. Andrew Murray, author of *The True Vine,* explains how the new graft becomes one with the vine: "When a new graft is placed in a vine and it abides there, there is a twofold process that takes place. The first is in the wood. The graft shoots its little roots and fibers down into the stem, and the stem grows up into the graft, and what has been called the structural union is effected. The graft abides and becomes one with the vine, and even though the vine were to die, would still be one wood with it. Then there is the second process, in which the sap of the vine enters the new structure, and uses it as a passage through which sap can flow up to show itself in young shoots and leaves and fruit. Here is the vital union. Into the graft which abides in the stock, the stock enters with sap to abide in it."[3]

▶▶▶ GOING DEEPER

When we abide in Christ we must expect to be pruned as the grapevine is pruned. The disciples were pruned, cleansed by the words Jesus spoke to them. Our cleansing may consist of hard times or discipline or seemingly impossible situations. As we grow ever more aware of abiding in Christ, we realize which of our habits and leanings are extraneous and harmful, which things in our lives draw us away from him. We must allow these things to be pruned away. This image of pruning, of cleansing, may also hearken back to the message of John the Baptist, "Repent, for the kingdom of heaven has come near" (Matt 3:2). It is impossible for God to work in our lives and for us to live in the fullness of

Have another member read this section.

God if we are unrepentant for the things we have done wrong, and we continue to commit those sins.

Next, we must abide in Christ in order to bear fruit. The apostle Paul expresses this truth another way: "The fruit of the Spirit is love, joy, peace, patience, kindness, generosity, faithfulness, gentleness, and self-control" (Gal 5:22–23). This is lasting fruit, fruit that is so winsome it will draw people to Christ through our example. The words of the Scripture Reading are aimed at the disciples of Jesus Christ, who had traveled with him for many long months and learned much. They had gone on missionary trips by themselves, where they were able to cast out demons, heal illnesses, and proclaim the kingdom of God. They had taken risks and been ridiculed. As disciples their lives had produced abundant fruit, a wonderful example for us.

Finally, we are to abide in Jesus's love. How is this done? While it is tempting to concoct a formula, we need to accept that what it means to abide with Christ will be different for each of us. As with any endeavor, if we are intentional in plan and action we will see results. And what is the proof that we are abiding in his love? First, we keep Jesus's commandments. As he said in Matthew 22:37–40, "'You shall love the Lord your God with all your heart, and with all your soul, and with all your mind.' This is the greatest and first commandment. And a second is like it: 'You shall love your neighbor as yourself.' On these two commandments hang all the law and the prophets." Keeping his commandments helps the life-giving sap of his love nourish our souls, so that we in turn can love him back and bring to all precious people his love and the message that the kingdom of God is available. Second, we experience a deep sense of joy. As the French mathematician and physicist Blaise Pascal wrote on a piece of paper that, after his death, was found sewn into the lining of his coat:

> "From about half-past ten in the evening
>   until about half-past midnight.
> Fire.
> The God of Abraham, the God of Isaac, the God of Jacob.
> Not of the philosophers and intellectuals.
> Certitude, certitude, feeling, joy, peace.
> The God of Jesus Christ . . .
> Forgetfulness of the world and of everything except God. . . .
> Oh just Father, the world has not known you,
>   but I have known you.

Joy, joy, joy, tears of joy. . . .
Jesus Christ. . . . Jesus Christ."[4]

When abiding in Christ, we also discover the secret of the easy yoke. "Come to me, all you that are weary and are carrying heavy burdens, and I will give you rest. Take my yoke upon you, and learn from me; for I am gentle and humble in heart, and you will find rest for your souls. For my yoke is easy, and my burden is light" (Matt 11:28–30). The easy yoke is the life of ease. In the midst of challenges, pressures, anxieties, and fears, nevertheless there is confidence, release, settledness, and security. Jesus is with us, and we are yoked to him, learning to live from him. This is the one liberating reality. This is abiding in Christ.

How have you experienced the joy of abiding in Christ?

REFLECTION QUESTION
Allow each person a few moments to respond.

▶▶▶ POINTING TO GOD

Watchman Nee is a wonderful example of what we can accomplish when we truly abide in Christ and Christ abides in us. He was born Nee Shu-tsu in southern China in 1903. At the age of seventeen, after hearing an evangelist speak, Nee Shu-tsu became a disciple of Jesus Christ. Although he had grown up despising preaching because of the Chinese preachers who were servile to European and American missionaries, Nee nonetheless became a preacher. As a teen he preached to his fellow students, and after he confessed his hidden sins and made amends with the people he had previously offended, his preaching started to produce results. With his commission confirmed, Nee Shu-tsu adopted the English name Watchman and the Chinese name To-sheng, which means "watchman's rattle," because he considered his calling to be to sound a warning during the night.

Watchman Nee became one of the most influential Chinese Christians of the twentieth century. In addition to preaching and writing numerous books, he established scores of local churches in spite of suffering from a number of physical problems—tuberculosis, angina pectoris, and chronic stomach problems—and encountering the expected rejection and opposition to his teaching. Finally, in 1952, he was imprisoned during the Communist Cultural Revolution. Sentenced to fifteen years in prison, he was never released and died there in 1972.

✍ Choose one member to read this section.

Among his writings, we find this description of what it means to abide in Christ:

> The operation of His life in us is in a true sense spontaneous, that is to say, it is without effort of ours. The all-important rule is not to "try" but to "trust," not to depend upon our own strength but upon His. For it is the flow of life which reveals what we truly are "in Christ." It is from the Fountain of life that the sweet water issues.
>
> Too many of us are caught *acting* as Christians. The life of many Christians today is largely a pretence. They live a "spiritual" life, talk a "spiritual" language, adopt "spiritual" attitudes, but they are doing the whole thing themselves. It is the effort involved that should reveal to them that something is wrong. They force themselves to refrain from doing this, from saying that, from eating the other, and how hard they find it all! It is just the same as when we Chinese try to talk a language that is not our own. No matter how hard we try, it does not come spontaneously; we have to force ourselves to talk that way. But when it comes to speaking our own language, nothing could be easier. Even when we forget all about what we are doing, we still speak it. It flows. It comes to us perfectly naturally, and its very spontaneity reveals to everyone *what we are*.
>
> Our life *is* the life of Christ, mediated in us by the indwelling Holy Spirit Himself, and the law of that life *is* spontaneous. The moment we see that fact we shall end our struggling and cast away our pretence. Nothing is so hurtful to the life of a Christian as acting; nothing so blessed as when our outward efforts cease and our attitudes become natural—when our words, our prayers, our very life, all become a spontaneous and unforced expression of the life within. Have we discovered how good the Lord is? Then *in us* He is as good as that! Is His power great? Then *in us* it is no less great! Praise God, His life is as mighty as ever, and in the lives of those who dare to believe the Word of God the divine life is manifest in a power not one whit less mighty than was manifest of old.[5]

In this passage we get a glimpse into Nee's soul as he contrasts abiding in Christ and abiding in self-effort. Nee's words make the same point as the Devotional Reading. Our outward actions always stem from our internal communion with the Lord. We must be cautious about focusing outward—attempting to control our outward behavior and to say the right things. Instead we are to walk with God. As a result, our outward actions will be natural and spontaneous expressions of "the life within."

▶▶▶▶▶ GOING FORWARD

Christ lives in us and we in him. It is miraculous. Christ sustains and nurtures us; we are tenderly cared for by God the Father. Any accomplishments of ours are all due to Christ, not to our own effort. God also prunes away that which is unnecessary and harmful in our lives. As we grow ever more aware of abiding in Christ, as we progress in our internal communion with him, our lives will produce fruit. This fruit includes not only the characteristics described in Galatians 5:22–23, "love, joy, peace, patience, kindness, generosity, faithfulness, gentleness, and self-control," but also fruit like that produced by Watchman Nee—the books he wrote, the churches he planted, the lives he touched. All fruit stems from our inward communion with God. We know that Christ abides in us; our task is to come closer, where we can be in constant communication with this indwelling Christ. The more constant our communion with this inner Light, the better we are pruned and the more fruit we are able to produce.

Have another person read this section.

Christ abides *in* us, and we *in* him. It is mysterious. As Andrew Murray writes, abiding in Christ is yet another divine mystery. "*In* . . . There is no deeper word in Scripture. God is *in* all. God dwells *in* Christ. Christ lives *in* God. We are *in* Christ. Christ is *in* us: our life taken up *into* His; His life received *into* ours; in a divine reality that words cannot express, we are *in* Him and He *in* us. And the words, 'Abide *in* me and I *in* you,' just tell us to believe it, this divine mystery, and to count upon our God the Husbandman, and Christ the Vine, to make it divinely true. No thinking or teaching or praying can grasp it; it is a divine mystery of love. As little as we can effect the union can we understand it. Let us just look upon this infinite, divine, omnipotent Vine loving us, holding us, working in us. Let us in the faith of His working abide and rest in Him, ever turning heart and hope to Him alone. And let us count upon Him to fulfill in us the mystery: 'Ye in me, and I in you'" (emphasis added).[6]

What do you think of Watchman Nee's statement that the Christian life— abiding in Christ—should be spontaneous and natural? How does your own experience support or challenge his statement?

REFLECTION QUESTION
Again, allow each member a few moments to answer this question.

Abiding in Christ

The LORD is my shepherd, I shall not want.
     He makes me lie down in green pastures;
he leads me beside still waters;
     he restores my soul.
He leads me in right paths
     for his name's sake.

Even though I walk through the darkest valley,
     I fear no evil;
for you are with me;
          your rod and your staff—
          they comfort me.

You prepare a table before me
     in the presence of my enemies;
you anoint my head with oil;
     my cup overflows.
Surely goodness and mercy shall follow me
     all the days of my life,
and I shall dwell in the house of the LORD
     my whole life long. (PS 23)

After everyone has had a chance to respond, remind them that this is the last lesson in the book and ask the group if they would like to continue meeting. If everyone agrees to continue, this would be a good time to discuss when to meet and what material to use. When everyone has shared, the leader asks the members to be silent for a few moments before leading them in reading the Closing Prayer aloud together.

TAKING IT FURTHER

ADDITIONAL EXERCISE

Another way of working to constantly be aware of abiding in Christ is what Frank Laubach called his Game with Minutes, in which he tried to turn his thoughts to God at least once a minute. Try to do this for a set period of time each day. Challenge yourself to keep playing the Game with Minutes for longer and longer periods of time. To help stay focused, post reminders of your Game with Minutes on the bathroom mirror, the kitchen sink, the refrigerator, your bureau, your computer.

ADDITIONAL RESOURCES

Kelly, Thomas R. *A Testament of Devotion.* San Francisco: HarperSanFrancisco, 1941.

Murray, Andrew. *The True Vine: Meditations for a Month on John 15:1–16.* Chicago: Moody Press, 1898.

Nee, Watchman. *Sit, Walk, Stand.* Fort Washington, PA: Christian Literature Crusade, 1971.

In what ways has God "pruned" your life in the past?

QUESTIONS

What are some of the habits or leanings in your life now that God might be seeking to prune?

Have you ever found yourself "acting" as a Christian, as Watchman Nee described? If so, explain.

NOTES

LEARNING FROM JESUS: AN OVERVIEW

1. Richard J. Foster and others, eds., *The Renovaré Spiritual Formation Bible* (San Francisco: HarperSanFrancisco, 2005), 1788.

CHAPTER 1: EXPECTING THE MESSIAH

1. Philip Yancey, *The Jesus I Never Knew* (Grand Rapids, MI: Zondervan, 1995), 52–53.
2. Joseph Telushkin, *Jewish Literacy* (New York: William Morrow, 1991), 545, available at http://www.jewishvirtuallibrary.org/jsource/Judaism/messiah.html.
3 Telushkin, *Jewish Literacy,* 545.
4 Geffrey B. Kelly and F. Burton Nelson, "Editors' Introduction," *A Testament to Freedom,* by Dietrich Bonhoeffer (San Francisco: HarperSanFrancisco, 1990), 35.
5 Kelly and Nelson, "Editors' Introduction," *A Testament to Freedom,* 15–44.
6 Foster and others, eds., *The Renovaré Spiritual Formation Bible,* 1789.
7. Denise Giardina, "Costly Grace," *Sojourners* (Sept./Oct. 2003).
8. "Oh, Come, Oh, Come, Emmanuel," *Lutheran Book of Worship* (Minneapolis, MN: Augsburg, and Philadelphia, PA: Board of Publication, Lutheran Church in America, 1978), hymn 34.

CHAPTER 2: AND THE WORD BECAME FLESH …

1. Saint Augustine, *Fifteen Books of Aurelius Augustinus, Bishop of Hippo, On the Trinity,* trans. Philip Schaff (New York: Christian Literature Publishing, 1890), 112–13, 114–15.
2. Roger L. Fredrikson, *The Communicator's Commentary: John,* ed. Lloyd J. Ogilvie (Waco, TX: Word Books, 1985), 32.
3. Fredrikson, *The Communicator's Commentary,* 30. See pp. 30–36 for a full discussion.
4. Richard J. Foster, *Streams of Living Water* (San Francisco: HarperSanFrancisco, 1998), 280. See pp. 277–81 for a full discussion.
5. Ellen Charry, "Spiritual Formation by the Doctrine of the Trinity," *Theology Today* (October 1997); available at http://www.findarticles.com/p/articles/mi_qa3664/is_199710/ai_n8758496.
6. Charry, "Spiritual Formation by the Doctrine of the Trinity."

CHAPTER 3: EXPERIENCING THE SECOND BIRTH

1. John Wesley, *Sermons on Several Occasions,* vol. 1 (New York: Carolton & Phillips, 1856), 154–60.
2. Mother Teresa, letter to Malcolm Muggeridge, available at http://www.touchstonemag.com/docs/issues/16.10docs/16-10pg35.html.

3. Malcolm Muggeridge, *Confessions of a Twentieth-Century Pilgrim* (San Francisco: HarperSanFrancisco, 1988), 13.
4. Malcolm Muggeridge, *Jesus Rediscovered* (Garden City, New York: Doubleday-Galilee, 1969), 47–48.

CHAPTER 4: REDEFINING BLESSEDNESS

1. Dallas Willard, *The Divine Conspiracy* (San Francisco: HarperSanFrancisco, 1998), 97–100, 106.
2. Willard, *The Divine Conspiracy,* 98–99.
3. Willard, *The Divine Conspiracy,* 116.
4. Willard, *The Divine Conspiracy,* 115.
5. Foster and others, eds., *The Renovaré Spiritual Formation Bible,* 1800.
6. *The Cokesbury Worship Hymnal,* C. A. Bowen, gen. ed. (Nashville, TN: Abingdon-Cokesbury, 1958), hymn 43.

CHAPTER 5: FREEING THE SABBATH

1. Virginia Stem Owens, *Looking for Jesus* (Louisville, KY: Westminster/John Knox, 1998), 188–90.
2. Martin Luther, *Preface to the Letter of St. Paul to the Romans,* trans. Bro. Andrew Thornton, OSB (Munich: Roger & Bernhard, 1972), available at http://ccel.org/l/luther/romans/pref_romans.html.

CHAPTER 6: FEASTING ON THE WORD

1. Frederick Buechner, *The Hungering Dark* (San Francisco: HarperSanFrancisco, 1969), 29–32.
2. C. S. Lewis, *The Best of C. S. Lewis* (New York: Macmillan, 1952), 358.
3. Mother Teresa, acceptance speech for the Nobel Peace Prize, Oslo, 1979, available at http://www.nobelprize.org/peace/laureates/1979/teresa-lecture.html.
4. Mother Teresa, acceptance speech for the Nobel Peace Prize.

CHAPTER 7: CONFRONTING THE POWERS

1. Richard J. Foster, *The Challenge of the Disciplined Life* (San Francisco: HarperSanFrancisco, 1985), 180–83.
2. Foster, *The Challenge of the Disciplined Life,* 186–87.
3. C. S. Lewis, *The Screwtape Letters* (San Francisco: HarperSanFrancisco, 2001), ix.
4. Foster, *The Challenge of the Disciplined Life,* 190.

CHAPTER 8: WELCOMING US INTO COMMUNITY

1. Dietrich Bonhoeffer, *Life Together: A Discussion of Christian Fellowship,* trans. John W. Doberstein (San Francisco: HarperSanFrancisco, 1954), 19–21.
2. Bonhoeffer, *Life Together,* p. 23.
3. Patrick J. Burke, "The Spirituality of Taizé," *Spirituality Today* 42, no. 3 (Autumn 1990), 233–45.
4. Burke, "The Spirituality of Taizé."
5. Burke, "The Spirituality of Taizé."
6. Foster and others, eds., *The Renovaré Spiritual Formation Bible,* 7.

CHAPTER 9: LIVING ABUNDANCE

1. Walter Brueggemann, "Enough Is Enough," *The Other Side* (Nov./Dec. 2001, 37, no. 6), 10–13.
2. Brueggemann, "Enough Is Enough."

3. Dorothy Day, *The Long Loneliness: The Autobiography of Dorothy Day* (San Francisco: HarperSanFrancisco, 1980), 33–34.
4. Dorothy Day, quoted in *Time* (New York, December 29, 1975).
5. Foster, *Streams of Living Water,* 165.

CHAPTER 10: BALANCING MARY AND MARTHA

1. Emilie Griffin, *The Reflective Executive* (New York: Crossroad, 1993), 13–14, 18–19, 166–67.
2. Parker J. Palmer, *The Active Life* (San Francisco: Jossey-Bass, 1990), 6.
3. Brother Lawrence and Frank Laubach, *Practicing His Presence* (Jacksonville, FL: Seedsowers/Christian Books, 1988), 56–57.
4. Lawrence and Laubach, *Practicing His Presence,* 71–73.
5. Foster and others, eds., *The Renovaré Spiritual Formation Bible,* 1789.

CHAPTER 11: BEARING THE CROSS

1. François Fénelon, *Talking with God,* trans. Hal M. Helms (Brewster, MA: Paraclete, 1997), 141–42.
2. Eugene Peterson, *The Message* (Colorado Springs, CO: NavPress, 2002), 1763–64.
3. Dallas Willard, *The Spirit of the Disciplines* (San Francisco: HarperSanFrancisco, 1988), 263.
4. Fénelon, *Talking with God,* 141.
5. Miriam Huffman Rockness, *A Passion for the Impossible: The Life of Lilias Trotter* (Grand Rapids, MI: Discovery House, 2003), 84.
6. Huffman Rockness, *A Passion for the Impossible,* 85.
7. Dietrich Bonhoeffer, "The Cost of Discipleship" in *A Testament to Freedom,* eds. Geffrey B. Kelly and F. Burton Nelson (San Francisco: HarperSanFrancisco, 1990), 313.
8. Thomas Aquinas, *Lectures on the Gospel of John,* cited in *Christianity Today* (September 2005), 94.

CHAPTER 12: ABIDING IN CHRIST

1. Thomas R. Kelly, *A Testament of Devotion* (San Francisco: HarperSanFrancisco, 1941), 3–4, 11–12.
2. Kelly, *A Testament of Devotion,* 13.
3. Andrew Murray, *The True Vine: Meditations for a Month on John 15:1-16* (Chicago: Moody Press, 1898), 11.
4. Marvin R. O'Connell, *Blaise Pascal: Reasons of the Heart* (Grand Rapids, MI: Eerdmans, 1997), 96.
5. Watchman Nee, *Sit, Walk, Stand* (Fort Washington, PA: Christian Literature Crusade, 1971), 31–32.
6. Murray, *The True Vine,* 11.

ACKNOWLEDGMENTS

The seeds of this book lie in the rich material found in *The Renovaré Spiritual Formation Bible,* so first we must acknowledge and thank the other editors of that project—Richard J. Foster, Gayle Beebe, Thomas C. Oden, and Dallas Willard. Lyle SmithGraybeal has greatly enriched this guide with both his enthusiastic wellspring of ideas and his patient editing. At HarperSanFrancisco Cynthia DiTiberio has also done a wonderful job with the editing of the manuscript. Michael G. Maudlin of HarperSanFrancisco, Richard J. Foster and Lyle SmithGraybeal from RENOVARÉ, and Kathryn Helmers of Helmers Literary Services first envisioned this series of spiritual formation guides, so we thank them for their support and encouragement as well as for the faith they had in us. Finally, we are especially grateful to our families, particularly our spouses, Phil Graybeal and Ryan Waterman, for their support, inspiration, and love.

Lynda L. Graybeal and Julia L. Roller

Grateful acknowledgment is made to the following for permission to reprint material copyrighted or controlled by them.

The Scripture quotations contained herein are from the *New Revised Standard Version Bible.* Copyright © 1989, 1993, by the Division of Christian Education of the National Council of the Churches of Christ in the United States of America. Used by permission. All rights reserved.

Excerpts taken from *The Challenge of the Disciplined Life: Christian Reflections on Money, Sex, and Power* by Richard J. Foster. Copyright © 1985 by Richard J. Foster. Used with permission of HarperCollins Publishers, 10 East 53rd Street, New York, NY, 10022-5299, www.harpercollins.com. Published in the UK and Commonwealth under the title *Money, Sex, and Power* and reproduced by permission of Hodder and Stoughton, Limited, 338 Euston Road, London, England, www.hodderheadline.co.uk.

WHAT IS RENOVARÉ?

RENOVARÉ (from the Latin meaning "to renew") is an infrachurch movement committed to the renewal of the Church of Jesus Christ in all its multifaceted expressions. Founded by best-selling author Richard J. Foster, RENOVARÉ is Christian in commitment, international in scope, and ecumenical in breadth.

In *The Renovaré Spiritual Formation Bible,* we observe how God spiritually formed his people through historical events and the practice of Spiritual Disciplines that is The With-God Life. RENOVARÉ continues this emphasis on spiritual formation by placing it within the context of the two-thousand-year history of the Church and six great Christian traditions we find in its life—Contemplative: The Prayer-Filled Life; Holiness: The Virtuous Life; Charismatic: The Spirit-Empowered Life; Social Justice: The Compassionate Life; Evangelical: The Word-Centered Life; and Incarnational: The Sacramental Life. This balanced vision of Christian faith and witness was modeled for us by Jesus Christ and was evident in the lives of countless saints: Antony, Francis of Assisi, Susanna Wesley, Phoebe Palmer, and others. The With-God Life of the People of God continues on today as Christians participate in the life and practices of local churches and look forward to spending eternity in that "all-inclusive community of loving persons with God himself at the very center of this community as its prime Sustainer and most glorious Inhabitant."

In addition to offering a balanced vision of the spiritual life, RENOVARÉ promotes a practical strategy for people seeking renewal by helping facilitate small spiritual formation groups; national, regional, and local conferences; one-day seminars; personal and group retreats; and readings from devotional classics that can sustain a long-term commitment to renewal. RENOVARÉ Resources for Spiritual Renewal, Spiritual Formation Guides, and *The Renovaré Spiritual Formation Bible*—books published by HarperSanFrancisco—seek to integrate historical, scholarly, and inspirational materials into practical, readable formats. These resources can be used in a variety of settings, including small groups, private and organizational retreats, individual devotions, and church school classes. Written and edited by people committed to the renewal of the Church, all of the materials present a balanced vision of Christian life and faith coupled with a practical strategy for spiritual growth and enrichment.

For more information about RENOVARÉ and its mission, please log on to its Web site (www.renovare.org) or write RENOVARÉ, 8 Inverness Drive East, Suite 102, Englewood, CO 80112-5624, USA.

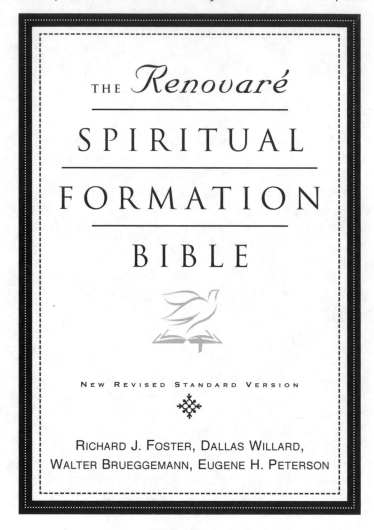